James S.M. Lynch

Ritus Ordinationum

Juxta Pontificale Romanum. Part 1

James S.M. Lynch

Ritus Ordinationum
Juxta Pontificale Romanum. Part 1

ISBN/EAN: 9783337038359

Printed in Europe, USA, Canada, Australia, Japan

Cover: Foto ©ninafisch / pixelio.de

More available books at **www.hansebooks.com**

RITUS

ORDINATIONUM

JUXTA

PONTIFICALE ROMANUM.

Curante Rev. J. S. M. LYNCH,
IN SEMINARIO PROVINCIALI APUD TROJAM, N Y. SACRÆ
LITURGIÆ PROFESSORE.

NEO-EBORACI, CINCINNATI, S. LUDOVICI.
BENZIGER FRATRES,
SUMMI PONTIFICIS TYPOGRAPHI.

1877.

Imprimatur,

✠ JOHN, CARDINAL McCLOSKEY
Archbishop of New York.

RITE OF ORDINATION.

Before the Ordination, the candidates for Orders put on the sacred vestments corresponding to the order to which they are to be promoted, to wit: those who are to receive tonsure carry a surplice folded on their left arm; those to be ordained to Minor Orders put on a surplice; those to be ordained to Subdeaconship put on an amice, alb, and cincture, and carry on their left arm the maniple and tunic; those to be ordained to Deaconship put on amice, alb, cincture, and maniple, and carry folded on their left arm a dalmatic and stole; those to be ordained to the Priesthood put on amice, alb, cincture, maniple, stole on their left shoulder after the manner of a deacon, fastened at the right side, chasuble folded on their left arm, and a white linen cloth fastened to the cincture. And each carries a lighted candle in his right hand.

Thus vested, at the proper hour, the candidates for Orders enter the church two by two, when each one takes the place assigned to him. When all have entered, the Bishop comes to the church, and approaching the middle of the altar, kneels down and prays for some time.

RITUS ORDINATIONIS.

Ante Ordinationem Ordinandi induunt habitum sacrum respondentem Ordini, ad quem sunt promovendi; videlicet tonsurandi superpelliceum replicatum brachio sinistro sustinent; Ordinandi ad Minores induunt superpelliceum; Ordinandi ad Subdiaconatum induunt amictum, albam, cingulum, brachio sinistro impositum ferunt manipulum ac tunicellam; Ordinandi ad Diaconatum induunt amictum, albam, cingulum, et manipulum brachio sinistro, in quo ferunt dalmaticam et stolam replicatam; Ordinandi ad Presbyteratum induunt amictum, albam, et cingulum, manipulum in brachio sinistro, stolam Diaconali more in humero sinistro, firmatam super latus dexterum, planetam replicatam super brachium sinistrum, sudarium albi coloris firmatum cingulo. Omnes vero manu dextera candelam ardentem gestant.

Sic induti Ordinandi hora competenti bini ac bini Ecclesiam ingrediuntur, ubi locum quisque sibi attributum occupant. Omnibus ingressis, Pontifex venit ad Ecclesiam, et accedens ante altare genuflexus ibidem aliquamdiu orat. Deinde

RITE OF ORDINATION.

He then goes to his seat, where he receives all the Pontifical vestments, after which Mass is begun.

Ordination.

After the Kyrie Eleison has been said,* the Bishop sits down, and the Archdeacon calls all those who are to receive orders, saying,

Let all come forward who are to be ordained.

The candidates for Orders leave their places and come before the altar, where they kneel in a semicircle. This is done if the size of the place and the number of the candidates permit; if not, they kneel in their places.

The Archdeacon, facing the candidates, reads from the Pontifical the inhibition or mandate, in the name of the Bishop, viz.:

† The Most Reverend in Christ— Father and Lord, His Lordship N. by the grace of God and of the Apostolic See, Bishop of N., orders and enjoins,

---

* It is supposed that the Ordination takes place during a low Mass. Should, however, a High Mass be celebrated, the usual ceremonies should be observed, and the prayers of the Ordination, instead of being read, should be sung.

† If the Ordination takes place outside of the prescribed times, there is first read the Apostolic mandate in which the faculty of ordaining is granted to the Bishop. This being read, the Bishop says: "Thanks be to God," and proceeds with the Ordination.

vadit ad sedem, ubi accipit omnia paramenta Pontificalia et statim Sacrum exorditur.

Ordinatio.

Dicto Kyrie Eleison * Pontifex sedet, et Archidiaconus vocat omnes ordinandos dicens :

Accédant omnes qui ordinándi sunt.

Ordinandi discedunt de locis suis et veniunt geniculatum ante altare quemdam efficientes semicirculum. Id vero fit, si loci amplitudo et numerus Ordinandorum patitur; sin minus genuflectunt loco ipso quem occupant.

Archidiaconus, conversus ad Ordinandos, legit ex Pontificali inhibitionem seu mandatum nomine Episcopi, videlicet :

† Reverendissimus in Christo Pater, et Dóminus Dóminus N. Dei et Apostólicæ Sedis grátia Epíscopus N., sub excommunicatiónis pœna præcipit et

---

* Supponitur Ordinationem fieri infra Missam privatam. Si autem celebretur Missa solemnis, consuetæ cæremoniæ servandæ sunt, et orationes Ordinationis non leguntur sed cantantur.

† Si Ordinatio fiat extra tempora, prius legitur mandatum Apostolicum cujus vigore Pontifici facultas conceditur ordinandi; quibus lectis, dicit Pontifex: " Deo Gratias," et ad ordinationem procedit.

under penalty of excommunication, on each and every one here present for receiving orders, that if any one of them perchance be irregular, or excommunicated by the canons or by his Superior, or interdicted, suspended, illegitimate, infamous, or otherwise excluded by the canons, or have come from another diocese without the permission of his Bishop, or have not been recorded, examined, approved and proclaimed, on no account shall he approach to receive Orders. And also that none of those ordained shall depart until after Mass is finished and the blessing of the Bishop received.

Ordination of Clerics.

After this, the Archdeacon calls those who are to receive tonsure, saying :

Let those come forward who are to be promoted to first tonsure.

The other candidates rise and return to their places, where they remain seated. Then the Notary

mandat ómnibus, et síngulis pro suscipiéndis Ordínibus hic præséntibus, nequis forsan eórum irreguláris, aut álias a jure, vel ab hómine excommunicátus, interdíctus, suspénsus, spúrius, infámis, aut álias a jure prohíbitus, sive ex aliéna Diœcési oriúndus, sine licéntia sui Epíscopi, aut non descríptus, examinátus, approbátus, et nominátus, ullo pacto áudeat ad suscipiéndos Ordines accédere. Et quod nullus ex ordinátis discédat, nisi Missa finíta, et benedictióne Pontíficis accépta.

De Clerico faciendo.

Post hæc Archidiaconus vocat tonsurandos, dicens;

Accédant qui promovendi sunt ad prímam tonsúram.

Ceteri Ordinandi consurgunt et redeunt sessum ad locum suum. Deinde vocantur omnes Tonsu-

calls the names of all those who are to receive tonsure, and each one answers,

Present.

They kneel in a semicircle before the Bishop, who sits on the faldstool, wearing his mitre.

The Bishop then rises, with his mitre on, and says:

V. Blessed be the name of the Lord.

℟. From henceforth, now and forever.

V. Our help is in the name of the Lord.

℟. Who made heaven and earth.

The Bishop then says:

Dearest brethren, let us beseech our Lord Jesus Christ for these his servants, who for his love hasten to receive tonsure, that he bestow upon them the Holy Ghost, who shall forever preserve them in the practice of a religious life, and shall protect their hearts from the evil ways of the world and from worldly desires, and that, as they are changed in their appearance, his right hand may grant them an increase of virtue, and, by opening their eyes, deliver them from all spiritual and

randi nominatim et sigillatim per Notarium, et quilibet respondet,

Adsum.

Quibus ante altare coram Pontifice in faldistorio cum mitra sedente genuflexis.

Pontifex surgit cum mitra, et dicit:

V. Sit nomen Dómini benedíctum.

℞. Ex hoc nunc, et usque in sæculum.

V. Adjutórium nostrum in nómine Dómini.

℞. Qui fecit cœlum et terram.

Oremus, fratres charíssimi, Dóminum nostrum Jesum Christum, pro his fámulis suis, qui ad deponéndum comas cápitum suórum pro ejus amóre festínant, ut donet eis Spíritum Sanctum, qui hábitum Religiónis in eis in perpétuum consérvet, et a mundi impediménto, ac sæculári desidério corda eórum deféndat; ut, sicut immutántur in vúltibus, ita dextera manus ejus virtútis tríbuat eis increménta, et ab omni cæcitáti spirituáli et humána óculos

human blindness, and bestow upon them the light of eternal grace. Who liveth and reigneth with God the Father in the unity of the same Holy Ghost, God, world without end. Amen.

After this, the Bishop sits, and the choir sings the following antiphon and psalm:

It is thou, O Lord, that wilt restore mine inheritance to me.

Psalm XV.

Preserve me, O Lord, for I have put my trust in thee. I have said to the Lord, Thou art my God, for thou hast no need of my goods.

To the saints who are in his land he hath made wonderful all my desires in them.

Their infirmities were multiplied: afterwards they made haste.

I will not gather together their meetings for blood-offerings: nor will I be mindful of their names by my lips.

The whole antiphon is repeated:

It is thou, O Lord, &c.

After the psalm has been begun, the Bishop with a small scissors cuts some hair from the head of each, in four places, namely, from the fore-

eórum apériat, et lumen eis ætérnæ grátiæ concédat. Qui vivit, et regnat cum Deo Patre in unitáte ejúsdem Spíritus sancti Deus, per ómnia sæcula sæculórum.

Post hæc, sedente Pontifice, schola inchoat et prosequitur antiphonam et psalmum:

Tu es, Domine, qui restítues hæreditátem meam mihi.

PSALMUS XV.

Conserva me, Dómine, quoniam sperávi in te : dixi Dómino : Deus meus es tu, quoniam bonórum meórum non eges.

Sanctis qui sunt in terra ejus, mirificávit omnes voluntátes meas in eis.

Multiplicátæ sunt infirmitátes eórum; póstea acceleravérunt.

Non congregábo conventícula eórum de sanguínibus: nec memor ero nóminum eórum per lábia mea.

Repetitur tota Antiphona :

Tu es Domine, etc.

Incepto psalmo, Pontifex cum forficibus incidit unicuique extremitates capillorum in quatuor locis ; videlicet, in fronte, in occipitio, et ad utram-

head, from the back of the head, and near each ear, and then some from the crown of the head; and he lets the cuttings fall into a dish. And each one while he is being tonsured says:

The Lord is the portion of my inheritance and my cup; it is thou that wilt restore my inheritance to me.

When all have been tonsured, the Bishop rises without his mitre, and turned towards the candidates, says:

Let us pray.

Grant, we beseech thee, O Almighty God, that these thy servants whose hair we have this day for thy love taken away, may remain perpetually in thy love, and that Thou keep them forever without stain. Through Christ Our Lord. Amen.

Then the choir sings the following antiphon and psalm. When it is begun the Bishop sits with his mitre on.

These shall receive a blessing from the Lord and mercy from God their Saviour; because this is the generation of them that seek the Lord.

que aurem, deinde in medio capitis aliquot crines capillorum, et in bacile deponit, et quilibet cum tondetur, dicit :

Dominus pars hæreditátis meæ, et cálicis mei : tu es, qui restítues hæreditátem meam mihi.

Omnibus tonsis, mitra deposita, surgit Pontifex, et stans versus ad illos, dicit :

Orémus.

Præsta, quæsumus omnípotens Deus, ut hi fámuli tui, quorum hódie comas cápitum pro amóre divíno deposúimus, in tua dilectióne perpétuo máneant ; et eos sine mácula in sempitérnum custódias. Per Christum Dóminum nostrum. ℞ Amen.

Tunc schola inchoat, et prosequitur Antiphonam sequentem. Qua incepta, Pontifex sedet cum mitra.

Hi accípient benedictiónem a Dómino: et misericórdiam a Deo salutári suo : quia hæc est generátio quæréntium Dóminum.

Psalm XXIII.

The earth is the Lord's and the fulness thereof: the world and all they that dwell therein.

For he hath founded it upon the seas, and hath prepared it upon the rivers.

Who shall ascend into the mountains of the Lord; or who shall stand in his holy place?

The innocent in hands, and clean of heart, who hath not taken his soul in vain, nor sworn deceitfully to his neighbor.

He shall receive a blessing from the Lord, and mercy from God his Saviour.

This is the generation of them that seek him, of them that seek the face of the God of Jacob.

Lift up your gates, O ye princes, and be ye lifted up, O eternal gates; and the King of Glory shall enter in.

Who is the King of Glory? The Lord who is strong and mighty: the Lord mighty in battle.

Lift up your gates, O ye princes, and

PSALMUS XXIII.

Domine est terra, et plenitúdo ejus: orbis terrárum, et univérsi qui hábitant in eo.

Quia ipse super mária fundávit cum; et super flúmina præparávit eum.

Quis ascéndet in montem Dómini? aut quis stabit in loco sancto ejus?

Innocens mánibus, et mundo corde, qui non accépit in vano ánimam suam, nec jurávit in dolo próximo suo.

Hic accípiet benedictiónem a Dómino; et misericórdiam a Deo salutári suo.

Hæc est generátio quæréntium eum, quæréntium fáciem Dei Jacob.

Attóllite portas, príncipes, vestras et elevámini portæ æternáles : et introíbit Rex glóriæ.

Quis est iste Rex glóriæ? Dóminus fortis, et potens : Dóminus potens in prælio.

Attóllite portas, príncipes, vestras, et

be ye lifted up, O eternal gates; and the King of Glory shall enter in.

Who is this King of Glory? the Lord of hosts he is the King of Glory.

Glory be to the Father and to the Son and to the Holy Ghost. As it was in the beginning, now and ever shall be, world without end. Amen.

Then the whole antiphon is repeated:

These shall receive, &c.

When this is finished the Bishop rises with his mitre on and turned toward the altar, says:

Let us pray.

And the ministers say:

Let us bend our knees.
℞. Rise up.

And then the Bishop turning toward those who have been tonsured, and who are still kneeling, says:

Listen, O Lord, to our supplications and vouchsafe to bless these thy servants whom in thy holy name we invest with this habit of holy religion,

elevámini portæ æternáles: et introíbit Rex glóriæ,
Quis est iste Rex glóriæ? Dóminus virtútem ipse est Rex glóriæ.
Glória Patri, et Fílio: et Spirítui Sancto. Sicut erat in princípio, et nunc, et semper: et in sæcula sæculórum. Amen.

Deinde repetitur tota Antiphona:

Hi accípient, etc.

Qua finita, surgit sine mitra Pontifex, et ad altare conversus, dicit:

Orémus.

Et ministri dicunt:

Flectámus génua.
℟. Leváte.

Et mox ad tonsos genuflexos versus Pontifex, dicit:

Adesto, Dómine, supplicatiónibus nostris, et hos fámulos tuos bene-✝dícere dignáre, quibus in tuo sancto nómine hábitum sacræ religiónis impó-

that, with thine aid, they may be worthy to remain always devout in thy church, and receive eternal life. Through Christ Our Lord. ℟. Amen.

Then the Bishop sits with his mitre on, and taking from each one his surplice, puts it on him, saying:

May the Lord put on thee the new man, who according to God is created in justice and in the holiness of truth.

The Bishop then rises without his mitre, and turned toward the candidates, says:

Let us pray.

O Almighty and Eternal God, be merciful to us sinners, and release these thy servants from every bond of worldly dress; grant that, while they put off the ignominy of a worldly garment, they may enjoy thy grace for evermore; and that as we make them bear on their heads the likeness of thy crown, so by thy strength they may deserve to obtain the eternal inheritance in their hearts. Who with the Father and the

nimus, ut, te largiénte, et devóti in Ecclésia tua persístere; et vitam percípere mereántur ætérnam. Per Christum Dóminum nostrum. ℟. Amen.

Tum Pontifex sedet cum mitra, et acceptum a singulis superpelliceum cuilibet imponit, dicens:

Induat te Dóminus novum hóminem, qui secúndum Deum creátus est in justítia, et sanctitáte veritátis.

Quo expedito, sine mitra surgit Pontifex et versus ad illos dicit:

Orémus.

Omnipotens sempitérne Deus, propitiáre peccátis nostris, et ab omni servitúte sæculáris hábitus hos fámulos tuos emúnda; ut, dum ignomíniam sæculáris hábitus depónunt, tua semper in ævum grátia perfruántur; ut sicut similitúdinem corónæ tuæ eos gestáre fácimus in capítibus, sic tua virtúte hæreditátem súbsequi mereántur ætérnam in córdibus. Qui cum Patre, et

Holy Ghost liveth and reigneth God, world without end. Amen.

Then the Bishop sits with his mitre on and addresses them in these words:

Dearest children, you ought to consider, that to-day you have come under the jurisdiction of the Church, and have obtained the privileges of clerks. Take care lest you lose them on account of your faults; and by a becoming exterior, good morals and works, endeavor to please God. Which may he grant through his Holy Spirit. ℟. Amen.

Then, at the direction of the Archdeacon, they return to their places.

Ordination of Porters.

The clerks being ordained, the Bishop rises without his mitre, goes to the Missal, and says:

Let us pray.

The assistants say:

Let us bend our knees.
℟. Rise up.

Spíritu Sancto vivis et regnas Deus, per ómnia sæcula sæculórum. ℟. Amen.

Deinde sedet cum mitra Pontifex, et alloquitur eos sub his verbis:

Filii charíssimi, animadvértere debétis, quod hódie de foro Ecclésiæ facti estis, et privilégia Clericália sortíti estis. Cavéte ígitur, ne propter culpas vestras illa perdátis; et hábitu honésto, bonísque móribus, atque opéribus Deo placére studeátis: Quod ipse vobis concédat per Spíritum sanctum suum. ℟. Amen.

Tum, suggerente Archidiacono, Ordinati redeunt ad loca sua.

De Ordinatione Ostiariorum.

Clericis ordinatis, Pontifex dimissa mitra assurgit, accedit ad Missale, et dicit:

Orémus.

Assistentes autem:

Flectámus génua.

℟. Leváte.

He then reads the first prayer and first lesson, which being read, the Bishop sits down with his mitre on. The Archdeacon calls the candidates, saying:

Let those come forward who are to be ordained to the office of Porters.

And the Notary calls them separately by name, and each one answers:

Present.

All being on their knees before the Bishop, he exhorts them, saying:

Dearest children, who are about to receive the office of Porters, observe what you must do in the House of God. It is the duty of the Porter to strike the cymbal and ring the bell, to open the church and the sanctuary, and the book for him who preaches. Be on your guard, therefore, lest through your negligence anything in the church be destroyed; open the house of God at certain hours for the faithful, and always close it to infidels.

Endeavor, also, that as you open and close with material keys the visible church, in like manner to close to the

Legit orationem primam et primam lectionem. Qua lecta, Pontifex sedet cum mitra. Archidiaconus vocat ordinandos dicens:

Accédant, qui ordinándi sunt ad offícium Ostiariórum.

Et mox Notarius singulos nominatim vocat et quilibet respondet:

Adsum.

Omnibus coram Pontifice genuflexis, admonet illos dicens:

Susceptúri, filii charíssimi, offícium Ostiariórum, vidéte, quæ in domo Dei ágere debeátis. Ostiárium opórtet percútere cymbalum, et cámpanam ; aperíre Ecclésiam, et sacrárium ; et librum aperíre ei qui prædicat. Providéte ígitur, ne per negligéntiam vestram, illárum rerum, quæ intra Ecclésiam sunt, áliquid depéreat ; certísque horis domum Dei aperiátis fidélibus : et semper claudátis infidélibus.

Studéte etiam, ut, sicut materiálibus clávibus Ecclésiam visíbilem aperítis, et cláuditis ; sic, et invisíbilem Dei Do-

devil and open to God, by your word and example, the invisible house of God, namely, the hearts of the faithful, so that the divine word which they hear, they may retain in their hearts and carry out in their lives, which may the Lord, through his mercy, accomplish in you.

Then the Bishop takes and presents to all, the keys of the church, which one after another they touch with their right hand, while the Bishop says:

Conduct yourselves as having to render an account to God for those things which are kept under these keys.

After this, the Archdeacon, or some one taking the place of the Archdeacon, conducts them to the door of the church, and makes them shut and open it; then he leads them to the tower, and presenting to each the bell-rope, directs him to ring the bell with one stroke; but if the tower be too distant and difficult of ascent, he makes each ring a little bell placed at the door of the church. Then he brings them back to the Bishop. When they are again kneeling before him, the Bishop, standing with his mitre on, and turned toward the candidates, says:

Dearest brethren, let us humbly beseech God the Father Almighty, to

mum, corda scílicet fidélium, dictis et exémplis vestris claudátis diábolo, et aperiátis Deo; ut divína verba, quæ audíerint, corde retíneant, et ópere cómpleant, quod in vobis Dóminus perfíciat per misericórdiam suam.

Deinde Pontifex accipit, et tradit omnibus claves Ecclesiæ, quas successive manu dextera singuli tangunt, Pontifice dicente:

Sic ágite, quasi redditúri Deo ratiónem pro iis rebus, quæ his clávibus recludúntur.

Post hæc, Archidiaconus, sive alius Archidiaconi vice fungens, ducit eos ad ostium Ecclesiæ, quod facit illos claudere et aperire; deinde ducit eos ad turrim et singulis eorum tradens funem campanæ, jubet ipsos pulsare campanam uno tinnitu; quod si turris nimis distet, et difficili ascensu sit, facit ut singuli campanulam ad ostium Ecclesiæ appensam pulsent. Deinde illos reducit ad Pontificem, quibus coram Pontifice genua flectentibus, stans cum mitra Pontifex versus ad ipsos ordinatos, dicit:

Deum Patrem omnipoténtem, fratres charíssimi, supplíciter deprecémur, ut

vouchsafe to bless these his servants, whom he has deigned to choose for the office of Porters, that they may be most diligent in their care of the house of God, observing both day and night the different hours for invoking the name of the Lord, with the assistance of Our Lord Jesus Christ, who liveth and reigneth with him in the unity of the Holy Ghost, God, world without end. Amen.

Then the Bishop, still standing, having put off his mitre, and turned toward the altar, says:

Let us pray.

And the ministers say:

Let us bend our knees.

℟. Rise up.

And turned towards the candidates, who are still kneeling, and standing, without his mitre, the Bishop says:

O Holy Lord, Almighty Father, Eternal God, vouchsafe to bless these thy servants in the office of Porters, that, amongst the Janitors of the Church, they may be devoted to thy service, and amongst thy elect they

hos fámulos suos bene✝dícere dignétur, quos in offícium Ostiariórum elígere dignátus est; ut sit eis fidelíssima cura in domo Dei, diébus, ac nóctibus, ad distinctiónem certárum horárum, ad invocándum nomen Dómini, adjuvánte Dómino nostro Jesu Christo; Qui cum eo vivit, et regnat in unitáte Spíritus sancti Deus, per ómnia sæcula sæculórum. ℞. Amen.

Tum, mitra deposita, stans Pontifex, et conversus ad altare dicit :

Orémus.

Et ministri subjungunt :

Flectámus génua.
℞. Leváte.

Et statim versus ad illos genuflexos, stans sine mitra, dicit :

Domine sancte, Pater omnípotens, ætérne Deus, bene✝dícere dignáre hos fámulos tuos in offícium Ostiariórum: ut inter janitóres Ecclésiæ tuo páreant obséquio, et inter eléctos tuos, partem

may be worthy to receive a part of thy reward. Through Our Lord Jesus Christ, thy Son, who liveth and reigneth with thee in the unity of the Holy Ghost, God; world without end. Amen.

After this, at the direction of the Archdeacon, they return to their places.*

Ordination of Readers.

The Porters being ordained, the Bishop returns to the Missal,† reads the versicle which follows the first lesson, then the second prayer and second lesson; which being read, the Bishop sits with his mitre on, and the Readers are called by the Archdeacon, in this manner:

Let those come forward who are to be ordained to the office of Readers.

And their names are called by the Notary. When they are on their knees before him, the Bishop exhorts them, saying:

As you have been chosen, dearest

---

* If, however, the same persons receive immediately another minor order, they remain kneeling, and their names are not called again by the Notary.

† This is the manner observed on the Saturdays of the Ember days, when several lessons are said. How it takes place at other times can be learned from the Pontifical.

tuæ mereántur habére mercédis. Per Dóminum nostrum Jesum Christum Fílium tuum, qui tecum vivit, et regnat in unitáte Spíritus sancti Deus, per ómnia sæcula sæculórum. Amen.

Post hæc Ordinati, suggerente Archidiacono, redeunt ad loca sua.*

De Ordinatione Lectorum.

Ostiariis ordinatis, Pontifex redit ad Missale,† legit versiculum qui sequitur lectionem primam, subjungit deinde secundam orationem et legit lectionem secundam; qua lecta Pontifex sedit cum mitra et Lectores vocantur per Archidiaconum hoc modo:

Accédant qui ordinándi sunt ad officium Lectórum.

Et mox nominantur per Notarium. Quibus coram Pontifice genuflexis, Pontifex admonet eos, dicens:

Electi, fílii charíssimi, ut sitis Lectó-

---

* Si autem iidem, qui ordinati sunt, alium minorem ordinem immediate recipiant, ibidem remanent, et iterum per Notarium non nominantur.

† Hic modus servatur in Sabbatis Quatuor Temporum in quibus plures dicuntur lectiones. Quomodo autem aliis temporibus fiat, ex Pontificali cognosci potest.

children, to be readers in the house of God, understand and fulfill your office. For God is powerful, and can increase in you the grace of eternal perfection. It is necessary for the Reader to read for him who preaches, to sing the Lessons and to bless the bread and all the new fruits. Endeavor, therefore, to announce distinctly and clearly the words of God, namely, the holy lessons, in such a manner that the faithful may understand and be edified, and without any corruption of the text, lest the meaning of the divine lessons intended for the instruction of your hearers should, by your negligence, be perverted. And what you read with your lips believe in your hearts, and practice by your works, so that you may be able to teach your hearers equally by your word and by your example. Therefore, when you read, stand in a high place, that you may be heard by all, and be seen, exhibiting by your elevated position the necessity incumbent upon you of possessing virtue in an emi-

res in domo Dei nostri, officium vestrum agnóscite et impléte. Potens est enim Deus, ut áugeat vobis grátiam perfectiónis ætérnæ. Lectórem síquidem opórtet légere ei qui prædicat; et lectiónes cantáre; et benedícere panem, et omnes fructus novos. Studéte ígitur verba Dei vidélicet lectiónes sacras, distíncte et apérte ad intelligéntiam et ædificatiónem fidélium, absque omni mendácio falsitátis, proférre; ne véritas divinárum lectiónum, incúria vestra, ad instructiónem audientium corrumpátur. Quod autem ore légitis, corde credátis, atque ópere compleátis; quátenus auditóres vestros, verbo páriter et exémplo vestro, docére possítis. Ideóque, dum légitis, in alto loco Ecclésiæ stetis, ut ab ómnibus audiámini et videámini, figurántes positióne corporáli, vos in alto virtútum gradu debére conversári; quátenus cunctis, a quibus audímini, et videmini, cœléstis

nent degree, and presenting the model of a heavenly life to all those by whom you are heard and seen, which may God accomplish in you, by his grace."

Then the Bishop takes and presents to all, the Book from which they are to read, which they touch with their right hand, while he says:

Receive (this book) and be readers of the Word of God, destined, if you faithfully and usefully fulfil your office, to have a part with those who from the beginning have acquitted themselves well in the ministry of the divine Word.

When this has been done, the Bishop, standing with his mitre on, turned toward the candidates, who are still kneeling, says:

Dearest brethren, let us beseech God, the Father Almighty, to mercifully bestow his blessing upon these his servants, whom he has vouchsafed to choose to the Order of Readers, that they may read distinctly what is to be read in the Church of God, and put in practice what they read, by their works. Through Our Lord Jesus

vitæ formam præbeátis; quod in vobis Deus ímpleat per grátiam suam.

Deinde Pontifex accipit, et tradit omnibus Codicem, de quo lecturi sunt, quem manu dextra tangunt, dicens:

Accípite et estóte verbi Dei relatóres, habitúri, si fidéliter et utíliter implevéritis offícium vestrum, partem cum iis, qui verbum Dei bene administravérunt ab inítio.

Quibus expeditis, et illis genuflexis, Pontifex stans cum mitra versus ad eos, dicit:

Oremus, fratres caríssimi, Deum Patrem omnipoténtem, ut super hos fámulos suos, quos in órdinem Lectórum dignátur assúmere, bene ✠ dictiónem suam cleménter effúndat; quátenus distíncte legant, quæ in Ecclésia Dei legénda sunt, et eádem opéribus ímpleant. Per Dóminum nostrum Je

Christ, his Son, who liveth and reigneth with him in the unity of the Holy Ghost, God, world without end. Amen.

Then the Bishop, putting off the mitre, and standing turned toward the altar, says:

Let us pray.

And the ministers say:

Let us bend our knees.

℟. Rise up.

Then, wearing his mitre, and turning towards the candidates, who are still kneeling, he says:

O Holy Lord, Almighty Father, Eternal God, vouchsafe to bless these thy servants in the office of Readers, that, instructed by their diligent reading of the Lessons, and making their lives conformable therewith, they may declare what is to be done, and do the same themselves, and so in both ways, by the example of their sanctity, be advantageous to the Holy Church. Through Our Lord Jesus Christ, thy Son, who liveth and reigneth with thee in the unity of the Holy Ghost, God, world without end. Amen.

sum Christum Fílium suum, qui cum eo vivit, et regnat in unitáte Spíritus sancti Deus, per ómnia sæcula sæculórum. ℟. Amen.

Tum Pontifex, mitra deposita, stans conversus ad altare, dicit:

Orémus.

Et ministri subjungunt:

Flectámus génua.

℟. Leváte.

Deinde conversus ad Ordinatos genuflexos dicit, sine mitra:

Domine sancte, Pater omnípotens, ætérne Deus, bene☩dícere dignáre hos fámulos tuos in offícium Lectórum; ut assiduitáte lectiónum instrúcti sint, atque ordináti; et agénda dicant, et dicta ópere ímpleant; ut in utróque sanctæ Ecclésiæ, exémplo sanctitátis suæ, cónsulant. Per Dóminum nostrum Jesum Christum, Filium tuum, qui tecum vivit et regnat in unitáte Spíritus sancti Deus, per ómnia sæcula sæculórum. ℟. Amen.

After this, at the direction of the Archdeacon, those ordained return to their places.

Ordination of Exorcists.

The Readers being ordained, the Bishop goes to the Missal, reads the versicle after the second lesson, recites the third prayer and third lesson ; which being read, the Bishop sits with his mitre on.

The Exorcists are called in the ordinary manner by the Archdeacon, who says :

Let those come forward who are to be ordained to the office of Exorcists.

The Notary calls them by name separately.

When they are on their knees before him, the Bishop exhorts them, saying:

As you are about to be ordained, dearest children, to the office of Exorcists, you ought to understand what you receive. For it is the duty of the Exorcists to cast out devils, to tell the people that he who does not communicate must give way, and to pour the water in the service. You receive, therefore, the power of imposing your hands on the possessed, and by the im-

Postea, suggerente Archidiacono, redeunt Ordinati ad loca sua.

De Ordinatione Exorcistarum.

Lectoribus ordinatis, Pontifex accedit ad Missale, legit versiculum post lectionem secundam, recitat orationem tertiam ac tertiam lectionem; qua lecta Pontifex sedet cum mitra.

Exorcistæ vero vocantur per Archidiaconum modo consueto, dicendo:

Accédant, qui ordinándi sunt ad Offícium Exorcistárum.

Et ipsi singulatim nominantur per Notarium.

Quibus coram Pontifice genuflexis, Pontifex admonet eos, dicens:

Ordinandi, fílii charíssimi, in offícium Exorcistárum, debétis nóscere quid suscípitis. Exorcístam étenim opórtet abjícere dæmones; et dícere pópulo, ut, qui non commúnicat, det locum, et aquam in ministério fúndere. Accípitis ítaque potestátem imponéndi manum super energúmenos, et per impositiónem mánuum vestrárum, grátia

position of your hands, with the grace of the Holy Ghost, and the words of the exorcism, the unclean spirits are expelled from the bodies of the possessed. Endeavor, therefore, that as you cast out devils from the bodies of others, in like manner you drive from your own minds and bodies all uncleanness and wickedness, lest you yield to those spirits whom by your ministry you drive away from others. Learn by your office to rule over your passions, so that the enemy may not be able to lay claim to anything as his own in your conduct. For then only will you rightly command devils in others, when you shall first have overcome their manifold wickedness in yourselves. May the Lord grant you to act thus, through his Holy Spirit.

After this, the Bishop takes and presents to all, the Book in which the exorcisms are written, which they touch with their right hands, whilst the Bishop says:

Take (this) and commit it to memory, and have power to impose hands

Spíritus sancti, et verbis exorcísmi pellúntur spíritus immúndi a corpóribus obséssis. Studéte ígitur, ut sicut a corpóribus aliórum dæmones expéllitis, ita a méntibus, et corpóribus vestris, omnem immundítiam, et nequítiam ejiciátis; ne illis succumbátis, quos ab áliis, vestro ministério, effugátis. Díscite per offícium vestrum vítiis imperáre; ne in móribus vestris áliquid sui juris inimícus váleat vindicáre. Tunc étenim recte in áliis, dæmónibus imperábitis, cum prius in vobis, eórum multímodam nequítiam superátis. Quod vobis Dóminus ágere concédat per Spíritum suum sanctum.

Post hæc Pontifex accipit, et tradit omnibus librum in quo scripti sunt exorcismi, quem manu dextera tangunt, Pontifice dicente:

Accípite, et commendáte memóriæ, et habéte potestátem imponéndi manus

on persons possessed, be they baptized or catechumens."

Afterwards, all continuing on their knees, the Bishop standing with his mitre on, says:

Let us humbly beseech, dearest brethren, God the Father Almighty to vouchsafe to bless these his servants in the office of Exorcists, that they may be spiritual rulers for expelling devils, with all their multiform wickedness, from the bodies of the possessed. Through his only begotten Son, Our Lord Jesus Christ, who liveth and reigneth with him in the unity of the Holy Ghost, God, world without end. Amen.

Then, turned towards the altar, and having put off his mitre, he says:

Let us pray.

And the ministers say:

Let us bend our knees.

℞. Rise up.

And immediately, turned toward the candidates, who are still kneeling, he says:

O Holy Lord, Almighty Father, Eternal God, vouchsafe to bless these

super energúmenos, sive baptizátos, sive catechúmenos.

Postea vero, omnibus devote genuflexis, Pontifex, cum mitra stans, dicit:

Deum Patrem omnipoténtem, fratres charíssimi, súpplices deprecémur, ut hos fámulos suos bene✠dícere dignétur, in offícium Exorcistárum, ut sint spirituáles imperatóres, ad abjiciéndos dæmones de corpóribus obséssis, cum omni nequítia eórum multifórmi. Per unigénitum fílium suum Dóminum nostrum, Jesum Christum, qui cum eo vivit, et regnat in unitáte Spíritus sancti Deus, per ómnia sæcula sæculórum. ℟. Amen.

Tum conversus ad altare, deposita mitra, dicit:

Orémus.

Et ministri subjungunt:

Flectámus génua.

℟. Leváte.

Et mox conversus ad Ordinatos genuflexos, dicit:

Domine sancte Pater omnípotens, ætérne Deus, bene✠dícere dignáre hos

thy servants in the office of Exorcists, that, by the imposition of hands, together with the words of the Exorcism, they may have power and authority to subjugate the unclean spirits, and also that they may be acceptable physicians of thy Church, confirmed by the gift of healing and by heavenly virtue, through Our Lord Jesus Christ, thy Son, who liveth and reigneth with thee in the unity of the Holy Ghost, God, world without end. Amen.

After this, at the direction of the Archdeacon, they return to their places.

Ordination of Acolytes.

The Exorcists being ordained, the Bishop returns to the Missal, and reads the versicle which follows the third lesson; then he reads the fourth prayer and the fourth lesson; which being read, he sits with his mitre on.

The Acolytes are called by the Archdeacon.

Let those come forward who are to be ordained to the office of Acolytes.

And the names are called by the Notary.

When they are kneeling before him, the Bishop exhorts them, saying :

fámulos tuos in offícium Exorcistárum ; ut per impositiónem mánuum, et oris officíum, potestátem, et impérium hábeant spíritus immúndos coercéndi ; ut probábiles sint médici Ecclésiæ tuæ, grátia curatiónum, virtutéque cœlésti confirmáti. Per Dóminum nostrum Jesum Christum Fílium tuum, qui tecum vivit, et regnat in unitáte Spíritus sancti Deus, per ómnia sæcula sæculórum. ℞. Amen.

Post hæc suggerente Archidiacono, redeunt ad loca sua.

De Ordinatione Acolythorum.

Exorcistis ordinatis, Pontifex redit ad Missale, et legit versiculum qui sequitur lectionem tertiam, deinde recitat quartam orationem et subjungit lectionem quartam ; qua lecta sedet cum mitra.

Acolythi vero vocantur per Archidiaconum:

Accédant qui ordinándi sunt ad offícium Acolythórum.

Et mox nominantur per Notarium.

Quibus coram Pontifice genuflexis, Pontifex admonet eos dicens :

As you are about to receive, dearest children, the office of Acolytes, reflect upon what you receive. For it is the duty of the Acolyte to carry the candlestick, to light the lights of the church, and minister wine and water for the Eucharist. Study, therefore, worthily to fulfill the office when you have received it. For you will not be able to please God, if carrying in your hands a light for Him, you serve the works of darkness, and by so doing set an example of faithlessness to others. But as Truth itself says: 'Let your light shine before men, that they may see your good works and glorify your Father, who is in Heaven (Matt. v, 16). And as the Apostle Paul says, " In the midst of a crooked and perverse generation, shine as lights in the world, holding forth the word of life " (Phil. ii, 15). Therefore let your loins be girt, and lamps burning in your hands that you may be children of the light (Jo. xii, 36). Cast off the works of darkness and put on the armor of light (Rom

Suscepturi, fílii charíssimi, offícium Acolythórum, pensáte quod suscípitis. Acólythum étenim opórtet ceroferárium ferre; luminária Ecclésiæ accéndere, vinum et aquam ad Eucharistíam ministráre. Studéte ígitur suscéptum offícium digne implére. Non enim Deo placére potéritis, si lucem Deo mánibus præferéntes, opéribus tenebrárum inserviátis, et per hoc áliis exémpla perfídiæ præbeátis. Sed sicut véritas dicit; Lúceat lux vestra coram homínibus, ut vídeant ópera vestra bona, et glorificent Patrem vestrum, qui in cœlis est (Matt. v, 16). Et sicut Apóstolus Paulus ait: In medio natiónis pravæ et pervérsæ, lucéte sicut luminária in mundo verbum vitæ continéntes (Phil. ii, 15). Sint ergo lumbi vestri præcíncti, et lucérnæ ardéntes in mánibus vestris, ut fílii lucis sitis (Jo. xii, 36). Abjiciátis ópera tenebrárum, et induámini arma lucis (Rom. xiii, 12).

xiii, 12). For you were heretofore darkness, but now light in the Lord. Walk then as children of the Light (Eph. v, 8). What that light is, upon which the Apostle so much, insists, he points out himself, adding: for the fruit of the light is in all goodness, and justice, and truth (Eph. v, 9). Be, therefore, solicitous, in all justice, goodness, and truth, to illumine yourselves and others and the Church of God. For then will you worthily minister wine and water in the sacrifice of God, when, by a chaste life and good works, you shall have offered yourselves as a sacrifice to God. Which may the Lord grant you through his mercy.

After this the Bishop takes and presents to all a candlestick with a candle not lighted, which one after another they each touch with their right hand, while the Bishop says:

Receive this candlestick and candle, and know that you are obligated to light the lamps of the church in the name of the Lord. ℞. Amen.

Erátis enim aliquándo ténebræ, nunc autem lux in Dómino. Ut fílii lucis ambuláte (Eph. v, 8). Quæ sit vero ista lux, quam tantópere incúlcat Apóstolus, ipse demónstrat, subdens: Fructus enim lucis est, in omni bonitáte et justítia, et veritáte (Eph. v, 9). Estóte ígitur sollíciti, in omni justítia, bonitáte, et veritáte; ut, et vos, et álios, et Dei Ecclésiam illuminétis. Tunc étenim in Dei sacrifício digne vinum suggerétis, et aquam, si vos ipsi Deo sacrifícium, per castam vitam, et bona ópera, obláti fuéritis. Quod vobis Dóminus concédat per misericórdiam suam.

Post hæc Pontifex accipit et tradit omnibus candelabrum cum candela extincta; quod succcssive manu dextera singuli tangunt, Pontifice dicente:

Accípite ceroferárium cum céreo, et sciátis vos ad accendénda Ecclésiæ luminária mancipári, in nómine Dómini. ℞. Amen.

Then he takes and presents to them an empty cruet, which likewise they touch, while he says to all:

Receive this cruet for supplying wine and water for the Eucharist of the blood of Christ, in the name of the Lord. ℞. Amen.

Afterward, they being still on their knees, the Bishop standing with his mitre on and turned toward them, says:

Let us humbly beseech, dearest brethren, God the Father Almighty, to vouchsafe to bless these his servants in the Order of Acolytes, so that, carrying a visible light in their hands, they may show forth a spiritual light in their conduct, with the assistance of Our Lord Jesus Christ, who with Him and the Holy Ghost liveth and reigneth God, world without end. Amen.

Then the Bishop, turning toward the altar, and standing without his mitre, says:

Let us pray.

And the ministers:

Let us bend our knees.

℞. Rise up.

Tunc accipit, et tradit eis urceolum vacuum, quem similiter tangunt, dicens communiter omnibus:

Accípite urcéolum, ad suggeréndum vinum, et aquam in Eucharistíam Sánguinis Christi, in nómine Dómini. ℟. Amen.

Postea eis genuflexis permanentibus Pontifex stans cum mitra versus ad eos, dicit:

Deum Patrem omnipoténtem, fratres charíssimi, supplíciter deprecémur, ut hos fámulos suos bene✝dícere dignétur in órdine Acolythórum; quátenus lumen visíbile mánibus præferéntes, lumen quoque spirituále móribus præbeant: adjuvánte Dómino nostro Jesu Christo, qui cum eo, et Spíritu sancto vivit, et regnat Deus, per ómnia sæcula sæculórum. Amen.

Tum Pontifex ad altare se convertens, deposita mitra, stans, dicit:

Orémus.
Et ministri:
Flectámus génua.
℟. Leváte.

And then the Bishop, turning toward the candidates, who are still kneeling, says:

O Holy Lord, Almighty Father, Eternal God, who, through Jesus Christ thy Son Our Lord, and his Apostles, didst send the light of thy glory into this world, and who, in order to blot out the ancient handwriting of our death, didst wish him to be fastened to the standard of the most glorious cross, and blood and water to flow from his side for the salvation of the human race, vouchsafe to bless these thy servants in the office of Acolytes, so that, in lighting the lights of thy church, and in offering the wine and water for the consecration of the blood of Christ Thy Son, in the Eucharistic sacrifice, they may faithfully minister at thy holy altars. Inflame, O Lord, their minds and hearts with the love of thy grace, so that, illumined with the sight of thy splendor, they may faithfully serve thee in the Holy Church, through the same Christ Our Lord. Amen.

Et mox Pontifex conversus ad eosdem genuflexos, dicit:

Domine sancte Pater omnípotens, aetérne Deus, qui per Jesum Christum Fílium tuum Dóminum nostrum, et Apóstolos ejus, in hunc mundum lumen claritátis tuæ misísti: quique ut mortis nostræ antíquum aboléres chirógraphum, gloriosíssimæ illum crucis vexíllo affígi, ac sánguinem, et aquam ex látere illíus pro salúte géneris humáni efflúere voluísti, bene ✠ dícere dignáre hos fámulos tuos in offícium Acolythórum; ut ad accendéndum lumen Ecclésiæ tuæ, et ad suggeréndum vinum, et aquam ad conficiéndum sánguinem Christi Fílii tui in offerénda Eucharistía, sanctis altaribus tuis fidéliter subminístrent. Accénde, Dómine, mentes eórum, et corda, ad amórem gratiæ tuæ, ut illumináti vultu splendóris tui, fidéliter tibi in sancta Ecclésia desérviant. Per eúmdem Christum Dóminum nostrum. ℟. Amen.

Let us pray.

O Holy Lord, Almighty Father, Eternal God, who didst speak to Moses and Aaron, and tell them to light the lamps in the tabernacle of the Testimony, vouchsafe to bless these thy servants, that they may be Acolytes in thy Church, through Christ Our Lord. Amen.

Let us pray.

O Almighty and Eternal God, fountain of light and origin of goodness, who, through Jesus Christ thy Son, the true Light, didst illumine, and by the mystery of his passion didst redeem the world, vouchsafe to bless these thy servants, whom we consecrate in the office of Acolytes, beseeching thy clemency to illumine their minds with the light of science, and water them with the dew of thy piety, so that, with thy assistance, their ministry may be acceptable, such that they may deserve to attain to an eternal reward, through the same Christ Our Lord. ℟. Amen.

Orémus.

Dómine sancte Pater omnípotens ætérne Deus, qui ad Móysem, et Aaron locútus es, ut accenderéntur lucérnæ in tabernáculo testimónii, bene ✠ dícere dignáre hos fámulos tuos : ut sint Acólythi in Ecclésia tua. Per Christum Dóminum nostrum. ℞. Amen.

Orémus.

Omnipotens sempitérne Deus, fons lucis, et orígo bonitátis, qui per Jesum Christum Fílium tuum, lumen verum, mundum illuminásti, ejúsque passiónis mystério redemísti, bene ✠ dícere dignáre hos fámulos tuos, quos in offícium Acolythórum consecrámus, poscéntes cleméntiam tuam, ut eórum mentes, et lúmine sciéntiæ illústres, et pietátis tuæ rore írriges ; ut ita accéptum ministérium, te auxiliánte, péragant, quáliter ad ætérnam remuneratiónem pervenire mereántur. Per eúmdem Christum Dóminum nostrum. ℞. Amen.

After this, at the direction of the Archdeacon, they return to their places.

Ordination of Subdeacons.

The Acolytes being ordained, the Bishop returns to the Missal and reads the versicle after the fourth lesson, then the fifth prayer and fifth lesson; which being read, the Bishop returns to his seat before the middle of the altar, and the Archdeacon, turned towards the candidates for Ordination, says:

Let those come forward who are to be ordained Subdeacons.

And the Notary calls each one of them, adding to the name and surname the title to which they are ordained; e. g., N. to the title of the Church of N.; Brother N., professed of the Order of N., to the title of poverty; N. to the title of the Mission; and so of others; and each one when he is called answers:

Present.

And they all come before the altar and remain standing two or three paces from the lowest step. And the Bishop, sitting with his mitre on, exhorts them (unless they are all religious, because then this exhortation is omitted), saying:

Dearest children, as you are about to be promoted to the Holy Order of

Post hæc, suggerente Archidiacono, Ordinati redeunt ad loca sua.

De Ordinatione Subdiaconi.

Acolythis ordinatis, Pontifex redit ad Missale, et legit versiculum post quartam lectionem deinde subjungit quintam orationem et lectionem quintam ; qua lecta Pontifex revertitur ad sedem suam, ante medium altaris et Archidiaconus versus ad Ordinandos dicit :

Accédant qui ordinándi sunt Subdiáconi.

Et Notarius unumquemque illorum vocat, nomini et cognomini adjungens titulum ad quem ordinantur ; *e. g.*, N. ad titulum Ecclesiæ N.; Frater N. professus Ordinis N. ad titulum paupertatis. N. ad Titulum Missionis, et sic de aliis, et quilibet vocatus dicit :

Adsum.

Et omnes procedunt ante altare, restantes longe ab infimo gradu passibus duobus tribusve ibique stant in pedes. Et Pontifex cum mitra sedens, admonet eos : (nisi omnes sint religiosi, quia tunc ista admonitio omittitur) dicens :

Filii dilectíssimi, ad sacrum Subdiaconátus Ordinem promovéndi, ite-

Subdeaconship, you should attentively consider, again and again, what a burden you this day freely seek. For as yet you are free, and it is optional for you to enter upon worldly pursuits; if, however, you receive this Order, you will no longer be at liberty to retrace your steps, but you will be obliged to serve God perpetually (to serve whom is to reign), and with his assistance to observe chastity and be forever bound to the service of the Church. Wherefore, while there is yet time, reflect—now if you wish to persevere in your holy resolution, in the name of God, come forward.

After the exhortation, the candidates advance one step toward the altar.

Then the Archdeacon calls the others who are to be ordained, saying:

Let those come forward who are to be ordained Deacons and Priests.

And they come before the altar, in such a manner, however, that those to be ordained to Subdeaconship kneel on the Epistle side, those to Deaconship on the Gospel side, and those to Priesthood in the middle before the altar, if this can be done conveniently, and if the number of the

rum atque íterum consideráre debétis atténte, quod onus hódie ultro appétitis. Háctenus enim líberi estis, licétque vobis pro arbítrio ad sæculária vota transíre; quod si hunc Ordinem suscepéritis, ámplius non licébit a propósito resilíre; sed Deo, cui servíre regnáre est, perpétuo famulári, et castitátem, illo adjuvánte, serváre oportébit, atque in Ecclésiæ ministério semper esse mancipátos. Proinde, dum tempus est, cogitáte, et, si in sancto propósito perseveráre placet; in nómine Domini, huc accédite.

Post admonitionem Ordinandi approximent uno passu ad altare.

Deinde Archidiaconus vocat cæteros Ordinandos, dicens:

Accédant qui ordinándi sunt Diáconi, et Presbyteri.

Et ipsi procedunt ante altare, eo tamen discrimine ut ordinandi Subdiaconatu genuflectant in latere Epistolæ, ordinandi Diaconatu in latere Evangelii, ordinandi autem Presbyteratu in medio ante altare, si potest id commode fieri et

RITE OF ORDINATION.

candidates permits; otherwise, they are placed in whatever way seems most convenient.

When they have been thus arranged, the Bishop, with his mitre on, kneels before the faldstool placed on the highest step, or on the platform of the altar, and all those who are to be ordained, prostrate themselves in their places on the carpet; the Ministers and the others present kneel; and the chanters intone the Litany of the Saints, the choir making the responses; or if the Office be celebrated without music, the Bishop recites the Litany, the ministers making the responses.

Lord, have mercy on us.
Christ, have mercy on us.
Lord, have mercy on us.
Christ, hear us.
Christ, graciously hear us.
God the Father of Heaven,
God the Son, Redeemer of the World,
God the Holy Ghost,
Holy Trinity, One God,
} *Have mercy on us.*

Holy Mary, *pray for us.*
Holy Mother of God, *pray for us.*

Holy Virgin of virgins,
St. Michael,
St. Gabriel,
St. Raphael,
} *Pray for us.*

si numerus ordinandorum patitur, secus disponuntur ut commodius videtur.

Quibus sic ordinatis, Pontifex, mitram in capite tenens, procumbit super faldistorium, in superiori gradu, sive plano altaris paratum, et omnes ordinandi in locis super tapetia prosternunt se; Ministri vero, et alii astantes genuflectunt; et schola inchoat Litanias, choro respondente; vel si Officium fiat sine cantu, Pontifex dicit Litanias Ministris respondentibus :

KYRIE, eleison.
Christe, eleison.
Kyrie, eleison.
Christe, audi nos.
Christe, exaudi nos.
Pater de cœlis Deus,
Fili Redemptor mundi Deus,
Spiritus Sancte Deus,
Sancta Trinitas, unus Deus,
} *Miserere nobis.*

Santa Maria, *ora pro nobis.*
Sancta Dei Genitrix, *ora pro nobis.*
Sancta Virgo Virginum,
Sancte Michael,
Sancte Gabriel,
Sancte Raphael,
} *Ora pro nobis.*

All ye holy Angels and Archangels,
All ye holy orders of Blessed Spirits,
St. John the Baptist,
St. Joseph,
All ye holy Patriarchs and Prophets,
St. Peter,
St. Paul,
St. Andrew,
St. James,
St. John,
St. Thomas,
St. James,
St. Philip,
St. Bartholomew,
St. Matthew,
St. Simon,
St. Thaddeus,
St. Matthias,
St. Barnabas,
St. Luke,
St. Mark,
All ye holy Apostles and Evangelists,

Omnes Sancti Angeli et Archangeli,
orate pro nobis.
Omnes Sancti Beatorum Spirituum
ordines, *orate pro nobis.*
Sancte Joannes Baptista, *ora pro nobis.*
Sancte Joseph, *ora pro nobis.*
Omnes Sancti Patriarchæ et Prophetæ,
orate pro nobis.
Sancte Petre,
Sancte Paule,
Sancte Andrea,
Sancte Jacobe,
Sancte Joannes,
Sancte Thoma,
Sancte Jacobe,
Sancte Philippe,
Sancte Bartholomæe,
Sancte Matthæe,
Sancte Simon,
Sancte Thaddæe,
Sancte Matthia,
Sancte Barnaba,
Sancte Luca,
Sancte Marce,
} *Ora pro nobis.*
Omnes Sancti Apostoli et Evangelistæ,
orate pro nobis.

All ye holy Disciples of our Lord,

All ye holy Innocents,

St. Stephen,
St. Laurence,
St. Vincent,
St. Fabian and St. Sebastian,
St. John and St. Paul,
St. Cosmas and St. Damian,
St. Gervase and St. Protase,
All ye holy Martyrs,
St. Sylvester,
St. Gregory,
St. Ambrose,
St. Augustine,
St. Jerome,
St. Martin,
St Nicholas,
All ye holy Bishops and Confessors,
All ye holy Doctors,
St. Antony,
St Benedict,
St. Bernard,
St. Dominic,
St. Francis,

RITUS ORDINATIONIS. 33

Omnes Sancti Discipuli Domini, *orate pro nobis.*
Omnes Sancti Innocentes, *orate pro nobis.*
Sancte Stephane,
Sancte Laurenti,
Sancte Vincenti,
Sancti Fabiane et Sebastiane,
Sancti Joannes et Paule,
Sancti Cosma et Damiane,
Sancti Gervasi et Protasi,
} *Ora, etc. Orate pro nobis.*
Omnes Sancti Martyres, *orate pro nobis,*
Sancte Sylvester,
Sancte Gregori,
Sancte Ambrosi,
Sancte Augustine,
Sancte Hieronyme,
Sancte Martine,
Sancte Nicolae,
} *Ora, etc.*
Omnes Sancti Pontifices et Confessores, *orate pro nobis.*
Omnes Sancti Doctores, *orate pro nobis.*
Sancte Antoni,
Sancte Benedicte,
Sancte Bernarde,
Sancte Dominice,
Sancte Francisce,
} *Ora pro nobis.*

All ye holy Priests and Levites,

All ye holy Monks and Hermits,

St. Mary Magdalen,
St. Agatha,
St. Lucy,
St. Agnes,
St. Cecilia,
St. Catharine,
St. Anastasia,
All ye holy Virgins and Widows,

} *Pray for us.*

All ye holy Men and Women, Saints of God,
Make intercession for us.
Be merciful.
Spare us, O Lord.
Be merciful.
Graciously hear us, O Lord.
From all evil, *O Lord, deliver us.*
From all sin, *O Lord, deliver us.*
From Thy wrath,
From a sudden and unprovided death,
From the snares of the devil,
From anger, and hatred, and all ill-will,

} *O Lord, deliver us.*

Omnes Sancti Sacerdotes et Levitæ, *orate pro nobis.*
Omnes Sancti Monachi et Eremitæ, *orate pro nobis.*
Sancta Maria Magdalena,
Sancta Agatha,
Sancta Lucia,
Sancta Agnes,
Sancta Cæcilia,
Sancta Catharina,
Sancta Anastasia,
} *Ora pro nobis.*

Omnes Sanctæ Virgines et Viduæ, *orate pro nobis.*
Omnes Sancti et Sanctæ Dei, *Intercedite pro nobis.*

Propitius esto.
Parce nobis Domine.
Propitius esto.
Exaudi nos Domine.
Ab omni malo, *libera nos, Domine.*
Ab omni peccato, *libera nos, Domine.*
Ab ira Tua,
A subitanea et improvisa morte,

Ab insidiis diaboli,
Ab ira, et odio, et omni mala voluntate,
} *Libera nos, Domine.*

RITE OF ORDINATION.

From the spirit of fornication,
From lightning and tempest,
From the scourge of the earthquake,
From plague, famine, and war,
From everlasting death,
By the mystery of thy holy Incarnation,
By thy coming,
By thy birth,
By thy baptism and holy fasting,

By thy cross and passion,
By thy death and burial,
By thy holy resurrection,
By thine admirable ascension,

By the coming of the Holy Ghost, the Comforter,
In the day of judgment,

} *O Lord, deliver us.*

We sinners, *beseech Thee to hear us*,
That thou vouchsafe to spare us,
That thou vouchsafe to pardon us,
That thou vouchsafe to bring us to true repentance,

} *We beseech, etc.*

A spiritu fornicatiónis,
A fulgure et tempestate,
A flagello terræmotus,

A peste, fame et bello,
A morte perpétua,
Per mysterium sanctæ Incarnatiónis tuæ,
Per advéntum tuum,
Per nativitátem tuam,
Per baptísmum et sanctum jejúnium tuum,
Per crúcem et passiónem tuam,
Per mortem et sepultúram tuam,
Per sanctam resurrectiónem tuam,
Per admirábilem ascensiónem tuam,
Per advéntum spíritus sancti parácliti,
In die judícii,

} *Libera nos, Domine.*

Peccatores, *Te rogamus, audi nos,*
Ut nobis parcas,
Ut nobis indúlgeas,

Ut ad veram pœniténtiam nos perdúcere dignéris,

} *Te rogamus, audi nos.*

That thou vouchsafe to govern and preserve thy holy Church,

That thou vouchsafe to preserve our Apostolic Prelate, and all orders in holy religion,

That thou vouchsafe to humble the enemies of thy holy Church,

That thou vouchsafe to give peace and true concord to all christian kings and princes,

That thou vouchsafe to grant peace and unity to all christian people,

That thou vouchsafe to confirm and preserve us in thy holy service,

That thou lift up our minds to heavenly desires,

That thou render eternal good things to all our benefactors,

} *We beseech Thee to hear us.*

Ut Ecclésiam tuam sanctam régere et conserváre dignéris,

Ut Domnum apostólicum, et omnes ecclesiásticos órdines in sancta religióne conserváre dignéris,

Ut inimícos sanctæ Ecclésiæ humiliáre dignéris,

Ut régibus et princípibus christiánis pacem et veram concórdiam donáre dignéris,

Ut cuncto pópulo christiáno pacem et unitátem largíri dignéris,

Ut nosmetípsos in tuo sancto servítio confortáre et conserváre dignéris,

Ut mentes nostras ad cœléstia desidéria érigas,

Ut ómnibus benefactóribus nostris sempitérna bona retríbuas,

Te rogamus, audi nos.

That thou deliver our souls and those of our brethren, relatives, and benefactors from eternal damnation,

That thou vouchsafe to give and to preserve the fruits of the earth,

That thou vouchsafe to give eternal rest to all the faithful departed.

} *We beseech Thee to hear us.*

Here the Bishop rises from his kneeling posture, and with his mitre on, turning toward those who are to be ordained, and holding in his left hand the crosier, says (the candidates, meanwhile, remaining prostrate):

That thou vouchsafe to bless these elect.

We beseech thee to hear us.

He says a second time:

That thou vouchsafe to bless and sanctify these elect. ℟. We beseech thee to hear us.

He says a third time:

That thou vouchsafe to bless, sanctify, and consecrate these elect. ℟. We beseech thee to hear us.

RITUS ORDINATIONIS.

Ut ánimas nostras, fratrum, propinquórum, et benefactórum nostrórum ab ætérna damnatióne erípias,

Ut fructus terræ dare, et conserváre dignéris,

Ut ómnibus fidélibus defúnctis réquiem ætérnam donáre dignéris.

Te rogamus, audi nos.

Hic surgit Pontifex cum mitra ab accubitu, et se ad Ordinandos vertens, et baculum pastoralem in sinistra manu tenens ordinandis prostratis manentibus, dicit:

Ut hos electos bene☩dícere dignéris.

Te rogámus audi nos.

Secundo dicit;

Ut hos eléctos bene☩dícere, et sanctificáre dignéris. ℞. Te rogámus, audi nos.

Tertio dicit:

Ut hos eléctos bene☩dícere, sanctificáre, et consecráre dignéris. ℞. Te rogámus, audi nos.

Then he kneels again before the faldstool, the chanters continuing the Litany to the end, as follows:

That Thou vouchsafe graciously to hear us, we beseech Thee to hear us.

Son of God, we beseech Thee to hear us.

Lamb of God, who takest away the sins of the world, spare us, O Lord.

Lamb of God, who takest away the sins of the world, graciously hear us, O Lord.

Lamb of God, who takest away the sins of the world, have mercy on us.

Christ hear us. Christ graciously hear us.

Lord have mercy on us.
Christ have mercy on us.
Lord have mercy on us.

The Litany being finished, the Bishop rises and sits on the faldstool before the middle of the altar with his mitre on, and the Archdeacon says in a loud voice:

Let those who are to be ordained Deacons and Priests retire to their places.

Tum iterum super faldistorium procumbit, schola perficiente Litanias usque ad finem, videlicet:

Ut nos exaudíre dignéris, te rogámus audi nos.

Fili Dei, te rogámus audi nos.

Agnus Dei, qui tollis peccáta mundi, parce nobis Dómine.

Agnus Dei, qui tollis peccáta mundi, exáudi nos, Dómine.

Agnus Dei, qui tollis peccáta mundi, miserére nobis.

Christe, audi nos. Christe, exáudi nos.

Kyrie, eleison.

Christe, eleison.

Kyrie, eleison.

Quibus finitis, Pontifex surgens cum mitra sedet super faldistorium ante medium altaris, et Archidiaconus dicit alta voce:

Recédant in partem, qui ordinándi sunt Diáconi, et Presbýteri.

RITE OF ORDINATION.

And all rise and return to their places except those who are to be ordained Subdeacons, who remain kneeling before the altar, and the Bishop exhorts them, saying:

Dearest children, who are about to receive the office of Subdeacon, consider well the ministry that is given to you. It is the duty of the Subdeacon to prepare water for the service of the altar, to wash the palls of the altar (antipendiums) and corporals, to assist the Deacon, and present him the chalice and paten used in the sacrifice. Of the offerings, called the bread of the proposition, which are brought to the altar, no more than what is sufficient for the people should be placed on the altar, so that nothing corrupt may remain in the sanctuary. The palls which cover the front of the altar (antipendiums) should be washed in one vessel, and the corporal palls in another; and none of the other linens should be washed in the vessel in which the corporal palls have been washed, and the water so used should be thrown into the *sacrarium*. Study, therefore, while executing neatly and most diligently

Et omnes consurgunt in pedes et redeunt ad loca sua, exceptis Ordinandis ad Subdiaconatum qui perstant nixi genibus ante altare et Pontifex admonet eos dicens:

Adeptúri, fílii dilectíssimi, offícium Subdiaconátus sédulo atténdite, quale ministérium vobis tráditur. Subdiáconum enim opórtet aquam ad ministérium altáris præparáre; Diácono ministráre; pallas altáris, et corporália ablúere; Cálicem, et Paténam in usum sacrifícii eídem offérre. Oblatiónes quæ véniunt in altáre, panes propositiónis vocántur: de ipsis oblatiónibus tantum debet in altáre poni, quantum pópulo possit suffícere, ne áliquid pútridum in sacrário remáneat. Pallæ, quæ sunt in substratório altáris, in álio vase debent lavári, et in álio corporáles pallæ. Ubi autem corporáles pallæ lotæ fúerint, nullum áliud lineámen debet lavári, ípsaque lotiónis aqua in baptistérium debet vergi. Studéte ítaque, ut ista visibília ministéria quæ

these visible services which we have indicated, in like manner, also, to perform those invisible ones, of which these are the exemplars. For the altar of the Holy Church is Christ himself, according to John, who, in his Apocalypse, relates that he saw a golden altar, Christ, standing before the throne (Apoc. viii, 3), in whom and through whom the offerings of the faithful are consecrated to God the Father. The palls of the altar (antipendiums) and corporals represent the members of Christ, namely, God's faithful, by whom the Lord, as with precious vestments, is robed, as the Psalmist saith: "The Lord hath reigned, he is clothed with beauty" (Psal. xcii, 1). Blessed John, also, in the Apocalypse, saw the Son of Man girded with a golden cincture (Apoc. i, 13), that is, with a multitude of saints. If, therefore, through human frailty, it should happen that the faithful in any way be sin-stained, you should present them the water of heavenly doctrine, purified by which, they may again become the ornament

díximus, nítide et diligentíssime compléntes, invisibília horum exémplo perficiátis. Altáre quidem sanctæ Ecclésiæ, ipse est Christus, teste Joánne, qui in Apocalypsi sua, altáre áureum se vidísse pérhibet, stans ante thronum, (Apoc. viii, 3) in quo, et per quem, oblatiónes fidélium Deo Patri consecrántur. Cujus altáris pallæ et corporália sunt membra Christi, scílicet fidéles Dei, quibus Dóminus, quasi vestiméntis pretiósis circúmdatur, ut ait Psalmísta : Dóminus regnávit, decórem indútus est (Psal. xcii, 1). Beátus quoque Joánnes in Apocalypsi vidit Fílium hóminis præcínctum zona áurea (Apoc. i, 13), id est, sanctórum catérva. Si ítaque humána fragilitáte contíngat in áliquo fidéles maculári, præbénda est a vobis aqua cœléstis doctrínæ, qua purificáti, ad ornaméntum altáris, et cultum divíni sacrifícii, rédeant. Estóte ergo tales, qui sacrifíciis divínis, et Ecclésiæ Dei, hoc est, córpori Christi

of the altar, and participate in the worship of the divine sacrifice. Be therefore such, that you may be faithful ministers in the divine sacrifices, worthily serving the Church of God, that is, the Body of Christ; be grounded in the true and Catholic faith, since, as the Apostle says, everything that is not of faith is sin, is schismatical, and is outside of the unity of the Church. And therefore, if heretofore you have been sluggish in devotion to the Church, henceforth you should be diligent; if heretofore you have been slumbering, henceforth you should be vigilant; if heretofore given to drink, henceforth temperate; if heretofore lacking in purity, henceforth chaste. All of which may he vouchsafe to grant you, who liveth and reigneth God, world without end. Amen.

> Then the Bishop takes and presents to all an empty chalice, with a paten placed on it, which one after another they touch with the right hand, while the Bishop says:

See whose ministry is given to

digne servíre valeátis, in vera et cathólica fide fundáti ; quóniam, ut ait Apóstolus ; Omne quod non est ex fide, peccátum est, schismáticum est, et extra unitátem Ecclésiæ est. Et ídeo, si usque nunc fuístis tardi ad Ecclésiam, ámodo debétis esse assídui. Si usque nunc somnolénti, ámodo vígiles. Si usque nunc ebriósi, ámodo sóbrii. Si usque nunc inhonésti, ámodo cásti. Quod ipse vobis præstáre dignétur, qui vivit, et regnat Deus in sæcula sæculórum. ℞. Amen.

Deinde Pontifex accipit, et tradit omuibus Calicem vacuum ; cum Patena vacua superposita, quem successive manu dextera singuli tangunt, Pontifice dicente :

Vidéte cujus ministérium vobis trá-

you; I admonish you, therefore, so to comport yourselves as to be pleasing to God.

<small>And the Archdeacon takes and presents to them cruets with wine and water, and a basin with finger towel, all of which things they likewise touch. Afterward the Bishop rises, and turned toward the people, and standing with his mitre on, says:</small>

Let us beseech God and our Lord, dearest brethren, to pour down his blessing and his grace on these his servants, whom he has vouchsafed to call to Subdeaconship, that, faithfully serving in his sight, they may obtain the rewards predestined for the saints, with the assistance of our Lord Jesus Christ, who liveth and reigneth with Him in the unity of the Holy Ghost, God, world without end. ℞. Amen.

<small>Then, putting off his mitre, and turned toward the altar, the Bishop says:</small>

Let us pray.

<small>And the ministers:</small>

Let us bend our knees.
℞. Rise up.

ditur; ídeo vos admóneo, ut ita vos exhibeátis, ut Deo placére possítis.

Et Archidiaconus accipit; et tradit eis urceolos cum vino, et aqua, ac bacile cum manutergio, quæ omnia similiter tangunt. Postea surgit Pontifex, et versus ad populum, stans cum mitra, dicit:

Orémus Deum, ac Dóminum nostrum, fratres caríssimi, ut super hos servos suos, quos ad Subdiaconátus offícium vocáre dignátus est, infúndat bene ✝ dictiónem suam, et grátiam; ut in conspéctu ejus fidéliter serviéntes, prædestináta sanctis præmia consequántur: Adjuvánte Dómino nostro Jesu Christo, qui cum eo vivit, et regnat in unitáte Spíritus sancti Deus, per ómnia sæcula sæculórum. ℞. Amen.

Tum deposita mitra, conversus ad altare Pontifex dicit:

Orémus.

Et ministri:

Flectámus génua.

℞. Leváte.

RITE OF ORDINATION.

And the Bishop, without his mitre, turned toward the candidates, who are still kneeling, says:

O Holy Lord, Almighty Father, Eternal God, vouchsafe to bless these thy servants, whom thou hast deigned to select for the office of Subdeacon, making them prompt and watchful sentinels of the heavenly army in thy holy sanctuary, and faithful ministers at thy holy altars, and let the spirit of Wisdom and Understanding, the spirit of Counsel and Fortitude, the spirit of Knowledge and Piety, rest over them, and fill them with the spirit of thy Fear, and confirm them in thy divine ministry, so that, obedient to thee, both in word and deed, they may obtain thy grace, through our Lord Jesus Christ, thy Son, who liveth and reigneth with thee in the unity of the same Holy Ghost, God, world without end. ℞. Amen.

Then the Bishop, sitting with his mitre on, draws the amice which hangs loosely on the neck of the candidates over the head of each, saying:

Et mox Pontifex versus ad Ordinandos genuflexos, dicit sine mitra:

Domine sancte, Pater omnípotens, ætérne Deus, bene ✠ dícere dignáre hos fámulos tuos, quos ad Subdiaconátus offícium elígere dignátus es; ut eos in sacrário tuo sancto strénuos, sollicitósque cœléstis milítiæ instítuas excubitóres, sanctísque altáribus tuis fidéliter subminístrent; et requiéscat super eos Spíritus sapiéntiæ, et intelléctus; Spíritus consílii, et fortitúdinis; Spíritus sciéntiæ, et pietátis; et répleas eos Spíritu timóris tui; et eos in ministério divíno confírmes, ut obediéntes facto, ac dicto paréntes, tuam grátiam consequántur. Per Dóminum nostrum Jesum Christum Fílium tuum, qui tecum vivit, et regnat in unitáte ejúsdem Spíritus sancti Deus, per ómnia sæcula sæculórum. ℟. Amen.

Tum Pontifex sedens, accepta mitra, amictum qui in collo ordinandorum jacet, imponit super caput singulis, dicens :

Receive this amice, by which is signified prudence in speech. In the name of the Father, and of the Son, and of the Holy Ghost. ℟. Amen.

Then he puts the maniple on their left arm, saying:

Receive this maniple, by which is signified the fruit of good works. In the name of the Father, and of the Son, and of the Holy Ghost. ℟. Amen.

After this he puts on each the tunic, and if there be but one tunic, he puts it on each one only as far as the shoulders, and then takes it off, leaving it on the last one, and saying to each:

May the Lord clothe thee with the tunic of sweetness and the garment of gladness. In the name of the Father, and of the Son, and of the Holy Ghost. ℟. Amen.

When all those Ordained have received these vestments, they return two or three together to the Bishop, who presents them the book of Epistles, which they touch with their right hand, while the Bishop says:

Receive this Book of Epistles and have power to read them in the Holy

Accipe amictum, per quem designátur castigátio vocis. In nómine Pa✠tris, et Fí✠lii, et Spíritus✠sancti. ℞. Amen.

Tum immittit manipulum in sinistrum brachium cuilibet, dicens:

Accipe manípulum, per quem designántur fructus bonórum óperum. In nómine Pa✠tris, et Fí✠lii, et Spíritus ✠sancti. ℞. Amen.

Post hæc induit quemlibet tunica, et si tantum unica sit, immittit illam cuilibet solum usque ad scapulas, ac retrahens postremum totaliter induit, dicens cuilibet:

Tunica jucunditátis et induménto lætítiæ índuat te Dóminus. In nómine Pá✠tris, et Fí✠lii, et Spíritus✠sancti. ℞. Amen.

Postquam induti sunt omnes Ordinati, redeunt junctim duo tresve ipsorum ad Pontificem qui tradit omnibus librum Epistolarum manu dextera ipsum simul tangentibus dicens:

Accípite librum Epistolárum, et habéte potestátem legéndi eas in Ecclésia

Church of God both for the living and for the dead. In the name of the Father, and of the Son, and of the Holy Ghost. ℟. Amen.

All these things being done, those Ordained, at the direction of the Archdeacon, return to their places.

Ordination of Deacons.

The Subdeacons being ordained, the Bishop goes to the Missal, and reads the canticle "Benedictus es" after the fifth lesson; then, in the middle of the altar, and turned towards the people, he says, "The Lord be with you," and turning to the Missal he reads the prayers. Afterwards, he reads the Epistle, and at the same time it is read by one of the newly ordained Subdeacons.

After the reading of the Epistle, the Bishop sits. The candidates for the Order of Deaconship are called by the Archdeacon, who says:

Let those come forward who are to be ordained to Deaconship.

And the Notary calls their names.

When they are all kneeling in a semicircle before the Bishop, the Archdeacon presenting them to him, says:

Most Reverend Father, Our Holy Mother the Catholic Church asks you

sancta Dei, tam pro vivis, quam pro defúnctis. In nómine Pá☩tris, et Fí☩lii, et Spíritus☩sancti. ℟. Amen.

Omnibus expeditis, suggerente Archidiacono, Ordinati redeunt ad loca sua.

De Ordinatione Diaconorum.

Subdiaconis ordinatis Pontifex accedit ad Missale, et legit canticum "Benedictus es," post lectionem quintam, deinde in medio altaris dicit "Dominus Vobiscum" ccnversus ad populum, et convertens ad Missale legit orationes. Postea legit Epistolam, et eodem tempore legitur per unum ex Subdiaconatis noviter ordinatis.

Lecta Epistola Pontifex sedet. Promovendi vero ad Ordinem Diaconatus per Archidiaconum vocantur, dicendo:

Accédant qui ordinándi sunt ad Diaconátum.

Et mox singulatim nominantur per Notarium.

Quibus in modum coronæ coram Pontifice genuflexis, Archidiaconus offerens illos Pontifici, dicit:

Reverendissime Pater, póstulat sancta Mater Ecclésia Cathólica, ut hos præ-

to ordain these Subdeacons here present, to the order of Deaconship.

The Bishop interrogates, saying:

Do you know if they are worthy?

The Archdeacon answers:

So far as human frailty permits to have knowledge of them, I know and testify that they are worthy of the burden of this office.

And the Bishop says:

Thanks be to God.

And he proceeds to ordain them. In the first place, the Bishop makes an announcement to the clergy and the people, saying:

With the assistance of the Lord God and our Saviour Jesus Christ, we choose these Subdeacons here present, for the Order of Deaconship. Should any one have anything against them, let him, for God's sake and for the honor of God, come forward with confidence and speak. Nevertheless, let him be mindful of his own condition.

And after a short pause, addressing himself to the candidates, he exhorts them, saying:

sentes Subdiáconos ad onus Diáconii ordinétis.

Pontifex interrogat, dicens:

Scis illos dignos esse?

Respondet Archidiaconus.

Quantum humána fragílitas nosse sinit, et scio, et testíficor ipsos dignos esse ad hujus onus offícii.

Et Pontifex dicit:

Deo grátias.

Et ad eorum ordinationem procedit. In primis Pontifex cum mitra sedens, clero, et populo annuntiat, dicens:

Auxiliante Dómino Deo, et Salvatóre nostro Jesu Christo, elígimus hos præséntes Subdiáconos in órdinem Diacónii. Si quis habet áliquid contra illos, pro Deo, et propter Deum cum fidúcia éxeat, et dicat; verúmtamen memor sit conditiónis suæ.

Et facta aliquali mora, Pontifex convertens sermonem suum ad Ordinandos, admonet eos, dicens:

Dearest children, who are about to be promoted to the Levitical order, consider earnestly to what a grade in the church you ascend. For it is the duty of the Deacon to minister at the altar, to baptize and preach. We know that in the old law, one of the twelve tribes, that of Levi, was chosen, which should be especially devoted to the service of the tabernacle of God and his sacrifices forever. And so great was the dignity conferred upon it, that no one unless of this tribe could be promoted to the ministry of this divine worship and obtain this office, so that, by a great and peculiar privilege of birthright, it deserved to be, and to be called the Tribe of the Lord. You hold to-day, dearest children, both the name and the office of this tribe, since you are chosen in the Levitical office for the ministry of the tabernacle of the testimony, that is, the Church of God, which, always equipped for battle, wages an incessant warfare against her enemies. Whence the

Provehendi, fílii dilectíssimi, ad Levíticum órdinem, cogitáte magnópere, ad quantum gradum Ecclésiæ ascénditis. Diáconum enim opórtet ministráre ad altáre, baptizáre, et prædicáre. Sane in véteri lege, ex duódecim, una Tribus Levi elécta est, quæ speciáli devotióne tabernáculo Dei, ejúsque sacrifíciis, ritu perpétuo deservíret. Tántaque dígnitas ipsi concéssa est, quod nullus, nisi ex ejus stirpe, ad divínum illum cultum, atque offícium ministratúrus assúrgeret; ádeo, ut grandi quodam privilégio hæreditátis et tribus Dómini esse mererétur, et dici: quorum hódie, fílii dilectíssimi, et nomen, et offícium tenétis, quia in ministérium tabernáculi testimónii, id est, Ecclésiæ Dei, eligimini in Levítico offício, quæ semper in procínctu pósita, incessábili pugna contra

Apostle says: "Our wrestling is not against flesh and blood, but against principalities and powers, against the rulers of the world of this darkness, against the spirits of wickedness in the high places" (Eph. vi, 12). You should carry this Church of God, as a tabernacle, and, robed in your sacred vestments, you should protect it by your divine preaching and perfect example. "Levi" signifies "added" or "assumed." Thus you, dearest children, who receive your name from the paternal inheritance, be free from carnal desires and worldly concupiscences which war against the soul; that you may be neat, clean, pure, chaste, as becomes the ministers of Christ and dispensers of the mysteries of God, so that you may be worthily added to the number of those in this ecclesiastical order, and may deserve to be the inheritance and the beloved Tribe of the Lord. And since you assist the priest in the sacrifice, and co-operate with him by distributing the Body and

inimícos dímicat: unde ait Apóstolus: Non est nobis colluctátio advérsus carnem, et sánguinem, sed advérsus príncipes, et potestátes, advérsus mundi rectóres tenebrárum harum, contra spirituália nequítiæ, in cœléstibus (Eph. vi, 12). Quam Ecclésiam Dei, véluti tabernáculum, portáre, et muníre debétis ornátu sancto, prædicátu divíno, exémplo perfécto. Levi quippe interpretátur ádditus, sive assumptus. Et vos fílii dilectíssimi, qui ab hæreditáte patérna nomen accípitis, estóte assúmpti a carnálibus desidériis, a terrénis concupiscéntiis, quæ mílitant advérsus ánimam; estóte nítidi, mundi, puri, casti, sicut decet minístros Christi, et dispensatóres mysteriórum Dei; ut digne addámini ad númerum ecclesiástici gradus: ut hæréditas, et tribus amá-

Blood of the Lord, be free from every allurement of the flesh, as the Scripture saith: "Be ye clean, you that carry the vessels of the Lord" (Is. lii, 11). Remember that Blessed Stephen was chosen to this office by the Apostles on account of his remarkable chastity. Be careful that to those to whom you announce the gospel with your lips, you present it also by live works, so that it may be said of you: "Blessed are the feet of them that preach the gospel of peace, of them that bring glad tidings of good things" (Rom. x, 16).

Have your feet shod with the examples of the Saints, in the preparation of the gospel of peace (Eph. vi, 15). Which may the Lord grant you by his grace. Amen.

Let a common prayer accompany a common desire that those who are prepared for the ministry of Deaconship may, by the prayers of the whole church, shine forth with the order of Levitical blessing, and, conspicuous

bilis Dómini esse mereámini. Et quia
commínistri, et co-operatóres estis
córporis, et sánguinis Dómini, estóte
ab omni illécebra carnis aliéni, sicut
ait Scriptúra: Mundámini, qui fertis
vasa Dómini (Is. lii, 11). Cogitáte
beátum Stéphanum, mérito præcípue
castitátis ab Apóstolis ad officium istud
eléctum. Curáte, ut quibus Evangélium ore annuntiátis, vivis opéribus ex-
ponátis, ut de vobis dicátur: Beáti
pedes evangelizántium pacem, evangelizántium bona (Rom. x, 16).

Habéte pedes vestros calceátos Sanctórum exémplis, in præparatióne Evangélii pacis (Eph. vi, 15). Quod vobis
Dóminus concédat per grátiam suam.
℞. Amen.

Commune votum, commúnis orátio
prosequátur; ut hi totíus Ecclésiæ
prece, qui ad Diaconátus ministérium
præparántur, Levíticæ bene✠dictiónis
órdine claréscant, et spirituáli conver-

by their spiritual life, they may be resplendent with the grace of sanctification, by the aid of our Lord Jesus Christ, who with the Father and the Holy Ghost liveth and reigneth, God, world without end. ℟. Amen.

Then the Bishop rising with his mitre on, and standing turned towards the candidates says, reading in a loud voice:

Let us, dearest brethren, beseech God the Father Almighty, mercifully to pour down upon these his servants, whom he has vouchsafed to choose for the Order of Deaconship, the grace of his blessing, and propitiously preserve in them the gifts of the consecration conferred upon them, and kindly hear our prayers, to graciously accompany with his favor what is to be done by our ministry, and sanctify and confirm with his blessing those whom, according to our judgment, we believe should be presented for the celebration of the sacred mysteries. Through His only begotten Son Our Lord Jesus Christ, who with Him and the Holy Ghost liveth and reigneth, God.

satióne præfulgéntes, grátia sanctificatiónis elúceant: Præstánte Dómino nostro Jesu Christo, qui cum Patre, et Spíritu sancto vivit, et regnat Deus in sæcula sæculórum. ℟. Amen.

Deinde surgens cum mitra Pontifex, stans versus ad Ordinandos, dicit, alta voce legendo:

Orémus, fratres caríssimi, Deum Patrem omnipoténtem, ut super hos fámulos suos, quos ad offícium Diaconátus dignátur assúmere, benedictiónis suæ grátiam cleménter effúndat, eísque consecratiónis indúltæ propítius dona consérvet, et preces nostras cleménter exáudiat; ut, quæ nostro gerénda sunt ministério, suo benígnus prosequátur auxílio: et quos sacris mystériis exequéndis pro nostra intelligéntia crédimus offeréndos, sua bene✠dictióne sanctíficet, et confírmet. Per unigénitum Fílium suum Dóminum nostrum Jesum Christum qui cum eo, et Spíritu sancto vivit, et regnat Deus.

Then, putting off his mitre, and extending his hands before his breast, he says:

World without end.

Amen.

The Lord be with you.

And with thy spirit.

Lift up your hearts.

We have lifted them up to the Lord.

Let us give thanks to the Lord our God.

It is meet and just.

It is truly meet, and just, right and profitable to salvation, that we should always, and in all places, give thanks to thee, O Holy Lord, Almighty Father, Eternal God, the giver of honors, dispenser of ranks, and disposer of offices, who, abiding in Thyself, renewest everything and arrangest all things, preparing with unceasing providence, and dispensing what is needful for various times, through thy Word, thy Power, and thy Wisdom, Jesus Christ, thy Son, our Lord; whose body, thy church,

Deinde, deposita mitra, extensis manibus ante pectus, dicit:

Per ómnia sæcula sæculórum.

℞. Amen.

V. Dóminus vobíscum.

℞. Et cum spíritu tuo.

V. Sursum corda.

℞. Habémus ad Dóminum.

V. Grátias agámus Dómino Deo nostro.

℞. Dignum et justum est.

Vere dignum et justum est, æquum et salutáre, nos tibi semper et ubíque grátias ágere, Dómine sancte, Pater omnípotens,ætérne Deus, honórum dator, ordinúmque distribútor, atque officiórum dispósitor, qui in te manens ínnovas ómnia, et cuncta dispónis per verbum, per virtútem, sapientiámque tuam, Jesum Christum Fílium tuum Dóminum nostrum, sempitérna providéntia præparas, et síngulis quibúsque tempóribus aptánda dispénsas. Cujus

diversified by a variety of heavenly graces, made up of distinct members bound together by the wonderful law that presides over the whole structure, thou grantest to grow and spread for the increase of thy temple. Thou who hast ordained in the service of a sacred charge a triple rank of ministers, to war for the glory of thy name, and didst choose in the beginning the sons of Levi to keep in perpetual ward the inheritance of eternal benediction, watching as faithful sentinels over the mystic movements within thy house. Look, also, we beseech thee, O Lord, with a benignant eye on these thy servants, whom with supplications we dedicate as deacons to the service of thy holy altars. We indeed, as men, devoid of divine perception and highest understanding, appraise their lives as far as falls within our power. But what is unknown to us eludes not thee, O Lord; hidden things escape thee not. Thou knowest all secrets, thou art the searcher of hearts,

corpus, Ecclésiam vidélicet tuam cœléstium gratiárum varietáte distínctam, suorúmque connéxam distinctióne membrórum, per legem mirábilem totíus compáginis unítam, in augméntum templi tui créscere, dilataríque largíris; sacri múneris servitútem trinis grádibus ministrórum nómini tuo militáre constítuens, eléctis ab inítio Levi fíliis, qui in mysticis operatiónibus domus tuæ fidélibus excúbiis permanéntes, hæreditátem benedictiónis ætérnæ sorte perpétua possidérent. Super hos quoque fámulos tuos, quæsumus, Dómine, placátus inténde, quos tuis sacris altáribus servitúros in offícium Diaconátus supplíciter dedicámus. Et nos quidem tamquam hómines divíni sensus, et summæ rationis ignári, horum vitam quantum póssumus, æstimámus. Te autem, Dómine, quæ nobis sunt ignóta non tránseunt, te occúlta non fallunt. Tu cognitor es secre-

thou art able to pierce into their lives with a heavenly discernment, which never fails thee, to blot out offences and to help them in all that they should do.

The candidates rise, and one after another go up to the altar and kneel before the Bishop, who places his right hand on the head of each, saying:

Receive the Holy Ghost in order that you may have strength, and to enable you to resist the devil and his temptations. In the name of the Lord.

The candidates, after the imposition of the Bishop's hand, return to their places before the altar and kneel.

Then the Bishop, holding his right hand extended, continues to the end of the Preface:

Send forth upon them, we beseech thee, O Lord, the Holy Spirit, to strengthen them with the gift of thy sevenfold grace, for the faithful execution of thy ministry. Let the practice of every virtue abound in them, mild

tórum ; tu scrutátor es córdium. Tu horum vitam cœlésti póteris examináre judício, quo semper prævales, et admíssa purgáre, et ea quæ sunt agénda, concédere.

Consurgunt Ordinandi : unus post alium ascendunt ad altare et geniculant ante Pontificem, qui singulis imponit capiti dexteram manum, dicens :

Accipe Spíritum sanctum, ad robur, et ad resistendum diábolo, et tentatiónibus ejus. In nómine Dómini.

Unusquisque post impositionem manus Pontificis redit ad locum suum ante altare et geniculat.

Deinde Pontifex prosequitur, extensam tenens manum dexteram, usque in finem Præfationis.

Emitte in eos, quæsumus, Dómine, Spíritum sanctum, quo in opus ministerii tui fidéliter exequéndi septifórmis grátiæ tuæ múnere roborentur. Abúndet in eis totíus forma virtútis, auctóritas modésta, pudor constans, inno-

authority, constant self-respect, the purity of innocence, and the observance of a spiritual life. In their conduct let thy precepts shine forth, so that the people may imitate the example of their virtue, and exhibiting the testimony of a good conscience, may they persevere, firm and steadfast in Christ, and by merited successes deserve, through thy grace, to rise from a lower grade to higher dignities.

What follows, he reads in a low voice, in such a manner, however, that he can be heard by those standing near him.

Through the same Jesus Christ our Lord, thy Son, who liveth and reigneth with thee in the unity of the Holy Ghost, God, world without end. Amen.

After this, the Bishop, sitting with his mitre on, puts the stole which each has in his hand on the left shoulder of each candidate kneeling before him, saying to each:

Receive this white stole from the hand of God, fulfill your ministry, for God is powerful to increase in you his

céntiæ púritas, et spirituális observántia disciplínæ. In móribus eórum præcépta tua fúlgeant, ut suæ castitátis exémplo imitatiónem sanctam plebs acquírat; et bonum consciéntiæ testimónium præferéntes in Christo firmi, et stábiles persevérent; dignísque succéssibus de inferióri gradu per grátiam tuam cápere potióra mereántur.

Quod sequitur dicit submissa voce legendo, ita tamen quod a circumstantibus possit audiri:

Per eúmdem Dóminum nostrum Jesum Christum Fílium tuum, qui tecum vivit, et regnat in unitáte Spíritus sancti Deus, per ómnia sæcula sæculórum. ℟. Amen.

Post hæc Pontifex sedens cum mitra cuilibet Ordinando ante se genuflexo, stolam quam singuli in manu habent, imponit successive super humerum sinistrum, dicens singulis:

Accipe stolam ✠ cándidam de manu Dei, adímple ministérium tuum: potens enim est Deus, ut áugeat tibi grá-

grace. Who liveth and reigneth, world without end. ℞. Amen.

He makes over each the sign of the cross, and both parts of the stole are immediately fastened on the right side of the candidate.

After this the Bishop, receiving the dalmatic, puts it on each successively; and if there be but one dalmatic, he puts it on each as far as the shoulder only, and leaves it on the last, saying to each:

May the Lord clothe thee with the garment of salvation and vestment of gladness; and may the dalmatic of justice encircle thee always. ℞. Amen.

The new Deacons all being vested, go up again to the Bishop, who presents to all the Book of Gospels or the Missal, which each touches, while the Bishop says:

Receive the power of reading the Gospel in the Church of God, both for the living and the dead. In the name of the Lord. Amen.

Which being done, the Bishop, standing, turned toward the altar, without his mitre, says:

Let us pray.

And the ministers:

Let us bend our knees.

℞. Rise up.

tiam suam: Qui vivit et regnat in sæcula sæculórum. ℞. Amen.

Deinde facit super quemlibet eorum signum crucis, et utraque pars stolæ statim cohibetur super latus dexterum Ordinati.

Post hæc Pontifex accipiens dalmaticam, induit ea quemlibet successive, et si tantum unica sit, immittit illam cuilibet solum usque ad scapulas, ac postremum totaliter induit, dicens cuilibet:

Induat te Dóminus induménto salútis, et vestiménto lætítiæ, et dalmática justítiæ circúmdet te semper: In nómine Domini. ℞. Amen.

Omnibus indutis novis Diaconis, iterum ascendunt ad Pontificem qui tradit omnibus librum Evangeliorum vel Missale, quem singuli tangunt, Pontifice dicente:

Accípite potestátem legéndi Evangélium in Ecclésia Dei, tam pro vivis quam pro defúnctis. In nómine Dómini. ℞. Amen.

Quo facto, Pontifex stans ad altare conversus dicit, sine mitra:

Orémus.

        Et ministri:

Flectámus génua.

℞. Leváte.

The Bishop turning toward those ordained, says:

Hear, O Lord, our prayers, and send forth the spirit of thy benediction upon these thy servants, that enriched by this heavenly gift, they may be able to obtain the favor of thy majesty, and to others set an example of living well. Through our Lord Jesus Christ, Thy Son, who liveth and reigneth with thee in the unity of the same Holy Ghost, God, world without end. Amen.

Let us pray.

O Holy Lord, Father of faith, hope, and grace, and rewarder of those who make spiritual advances, thou who, in the celestial and terrestrial ministries of angels everywhere taking place, dost diffuse the power of thy will through all the elements—vouchsafe to illumine these also, thy servants, with spiritual love, so that, devoted to thy service, they may grow up pure ministers at thy holy altars, and yet purer,

Et Pontifex vertens se ad ordinatos, dicit:

Exaudi, Dómine, preces nostras, et super hos Fámulos tuos Spíritum tuæ bene✠dictiónis emítte; ut cœlésti múnere ditáti, et tuæ majestátis grátiam possint acquírere, et bene vivéndi áliis exémplum præbére. Per Dóminum nostrum Jesum Christum Fílium tuum; qui tecum vivit, et regnat in unitáte ejúsdem Spíritus Sancti, Deus, per ómnia sæcula sæculórum. ℞. Amen.

Orémus.

Domine sancte, Pater fídei, spei, et grátiæ, et proféctuum remunerátor, qui in cœléstibus, et terrénis Angelórum ministériis ubíque dispósitis, per ómnia eleménta voluntátis tuæ diffúndis efféctum, hos quoque Fámulos tuos spirituáli dignáre illustráre afféctu; ut tuis obséquiis expedíti, sanctis altáribus tuis minístri puri accréscant; et indulgéntia tua puri\u00f3res, eórum gradu quos

through thy mercy, they may become worthy of the dignity of those seven whom thy Apostles, under the inspiration of the Holy Ghost, selected, and of whom Blessed Stephen was the first and leader. And thus, enriched with every virtue necessary for serving thee, may they be pleasing to thee. Through our Lord Jesus Christ Thy Son, who liveth and reigneth with thee in the unity of the same Holy Ghost, God, world without end. Amen.

Then, at the direction of the Archdeacon, they return to their places.

Ordination of Priests.

The Deacons being ordained, the Bishop returns to the Missal and reads the Tract as far as the last versicle, exclusively. Then, with his mitre on, he returns to the middle of the altar, where he sits upon the faldstool.

Then the Archdeacon calls the candidates, saying:

Let those come forward who are to be ordained to the Order of Priesthood.

Apóstoli tui in septenárium númerum, beáto Stéphano duce ac prævio, Spíritu sancto auctóre, elegérunt, digni exístant, et virtútibus univérsis, quibus tibi servíre opórtet instrúcti, tibi compláceant. Per Dóminum nostrum Jesum Christum Fílium tuum, qui tecum vivit, et regnat in unitáte ejúsdem Spíritus sancti Deus, per ómnia sæcula sæculórum. ℞. Amen.

Deinde suggerente Archidiacono, redeunt ad loca sua.

De Ordinatione Presbyterorum.

Diaconis ordinatis, Pontifex redit ad Missale et legit Tractum usque ad ultimum versiculum exclusive. Deinde cum mitra revertitur ante altare, ubi sedet super faldistorium.

Tunc Archidiaconus vocat Ordinandos dicens:

Accédant qui ordinándi sunt ad órdinem Presbyterátus.

And their names are read by the Notary, and they come up to the Bishop, and arrange themselves before him, in a semicircle.

Then the Archdeacon presents the candidates to the Bishop, saying:

Most Reverend Father, our Holy Mother, the Catholic Church, asks you to ordain these Deacons here present to the office of the Priesthood.

And the Bishop interrogates, saying:

Do you know if they are worthy?

The Archdeacon answers:

So far as human frailty permits to have knowledge of them, I know and testify that they are worthy of the burden of this office.

And the Bishop says:

Thanks be to God.

And he makes an announcement to the clergy and the people, saying:

Since, dearest brethren, both the master of a vessel and the passengers have either a common feeling of security or a common fear; in like manner, those who have a common interest should have a common opinion.

Ex mox nominatim leguntur per Notarium et illi ad Pontificem accedunt, et coram eo in modum coronæ se disponunt.

Tunc Archidiaconus præsentat ordinandos Pontifici, dicens:

Reverendíssime Pater, póstulat sancta mater Ecclésiæ Cathólica, ut hos præséntes Diáconos ad onus Presbytérii ordinétis.

Et Pontifex interrogat, dicens:

Scis illos esse dignos?

Respondet Archidiaconus:

Quantum humána fragílitas nosse sinit, et scio, et testíficor ipsos dignos esse ad hujus onus offícii.

Pontifex dicit:

Deo Grátias.

Et annuntiat Clero, et populo, dicens:

Quoniam, fratres charíssimi, rectóri navis et navígio deferéndis eádem est, vel securitátis rátio, vel commúnis timóris; par eórum debet esse senténtia, quorum causa commúnis exístit. Neque

For not uselessly indeed was it established by the Fathers that in the election of those who are to be employed for the ministry of the altar, the people also should be consulted, because what many may be ignorant of concerning the life and conduct of the candidate, is sometimes known to a few, and besides it is necessary in order that the faithful may the more readily yield obedience to him when ordained, whose ordination they sanctioned by their consent.

Indeed, so far as appears to me, the conduct of these Deacons, who, with the assistance of the Lord, are about to be ordained to the Priesthood, is commendable and pleasing to God, and worthy, in my opinion, of an increase of ecclesiastical honor. But lest one, or a few might be influenced by friendship, or prejudiced by affection, the opinion of many should be sought. Wherefore whatsoever you know of their conduct or morals, whatsoever you think of their merit, freely make known, and give them this testimony for the Priesthood

enim fuit frustra a Pátribus institútum, ut de electióne illórum, qui ad régimen altáris adhibéndi sunt, consulátur etiam pópulus: quia de vita, et conversatióne præsentándi, quod nonnúmquam ignorátur a plúribus, scitur a paucis et necésse est, ut facílius ei, quis obediéntiam exhíbeat ordináto, cui assénsum præbúerit ordinándo.

Horum síquidem Diaconórum in Presbyteros, auxiliánte Dómino, ordinandórum conversátio (quantum mihi vidétur) probáta, et Deo plácita exístit, et digna (ut árbitror) ecclesiástici honóris augménto. Sed ne unum fortásse, vel paucos, aut decípiat assénsio, vel fallat afféctio, senténtia est expeténda multórum. Itaque quid de eórum áctibus aut móribus novéritis quid de mérito sentiátis, líbera voce pandátis; et his testimónium Sacerdótii

as they shall deserve, and not from any motives of affection. Should any one therefore have anything against them, let him for God's sake and for the honor of God come forward and speak. Nevertheless, let him be mindful of his own condition.

Then the Bishop, after a short pause, addressing himself to the Candidates, exhorts them, saying:

Dearest children, who are about to be consecrated to the office of the Priesthood, endeavor to receive it worthily, and when received to discharge its obligations in a praiseworthy manner. For it is the duty of the priest to offer sacrifice, to bless, to govern, to preach, and to baptize. In truth, with great fear should one ascend to so great a dignity, and care should be taken that heavenly wisdom, approved morals and a long observance of the laws of God, should commend those selected for it. Wherefore, the Lord commanding Moses to choose seventy men from all Israel to help him, and who should share with

magis pro mérito, quam affectióne áliqua, tribuátis. Si quis ígitur habet áliquid contra illos, pro Deo, et propter Deum, cum fidúcia éxeat, et dicat; verúmtamen memor sit conditiónis suæ.

Deinde Pontifex, facta aliqua mora, convertens sermonem suum ad Ordinandos, admonet eos dicens:
Consecrandi, fílii dilectíssimi, in Presbyterátus offícium, illud digne suscípere, ac suscéptum laudabíliter éxequi studeátis. Sacerdótem étenim opórtet offérre, benedícere, præésse, prædicáre, et baptizáre. Cum magno quippe timóre ad tantum gradum ascendéndum est, ac providéndum, ut cœléstis sapiéntia, probi mores, et diutúrna justítiæ observátio ad id eléctos comméndent. Unde Dóminus præcípiens Móysi, ut septuagínta viros de univérso Israel in adjutórium suum elígeret, quibus Spíritus sancti dona divíderet suggéssit, quos tu nosti, quod

him the gifts of the Holy Ghost, added: "whom thou knowest to be ancients of the people" (Num. xi, 16). You indeed were typified in these seventy men and ancients, if, by the sevenfold Spirit, observing the Decalogue of the law, you shall be virtuous and perfect both in knowledge and in works.

Under the same mystery also, and the same figure in the New Testament, the Lord chose the seventy-two, and sent them two by two before him to preach, to show us at the same time by word and deed, that the ministers of his church should be perfect both in faith and works, grounded in the virtue of the twofold love, the love of God and the love of our neighbor. Such therefore strive to be, that, by the grace of God, you may be worthily chosen to assist Moses and the twelve Apostles, that is, the Catholic Bishops, who are prefigured in Moses and the Apostles. Truly, by this wonderful variety is the Holy Church encircled,

senes pópuli sunt (Num. xi, 16). Vos
síquidem in septuagínta viris, et sénibus
signáti estis; si per Spíritum septifór-
men, Decálogum legis custodiéntes,
probi, et matúri in sciéntia simíliter,
et ópere éritis.

Sub eódem quoque mystério, et
eádem figúra, in novo Testaménto,
Dóminus septuagínta duos elégit, ac
binos ante se in prædicatiónem misit;
ut docéret verbo simul, et facto, minístros Ecclésiæ suæ, fide et ópere debére
esse perféctos; seu géminæ dilectiónis,
Dei scílicet, et próximi virtúte fun-
dátos. Tales ítaque esse studeátis, ut in
adjutórium Móysi et duódecim Apostolórum, Episcopórum vidélicet catho-
licórum, qui per Móysen, et Apóstolos
figurántur, digne, per grátiam Dei, éligi
valeátis. Hac certe mira varietáte
Ecclésia sancta circúmdatur, ornátur,

adorned, and governed; since men in various orders are consecrated in it, some Bishops, others Priests of a lower order, Deacons and Subdeacons; and from many members, and of subordinate dignities, is constituted one body of Christ. Therefore, dearest children, chosen by the judgment of our brethren to be consecrated for our assistance, preserve in your conduct the integrity of a virtuous and holy life. Realize what you do, imitate what you handle, so that, celebrating the mystery of the Lord's death, you may be able to mortify in your members all inclination toward vice and concupiscence. Let your doctrine be spiritual medicine for the people of God; let the odor of your life be the delight of the Church of Christ, so that by your preaching and example you may build up the house that is the family of God, and so neither we for having promoted you, nor you for having received so great an office, may deserve to be condemned,

et régitur; cum álii in ea Pontífices, álii minóris órdinis Sacerdótes, Diáconi, et Subdiáconi, diversórum órdinum viri consecrántur; et ex multis, et altérnæ dignitátis membris unum Corpus Christi efficitur. Itaque, fílii dilectíssimi, quos ad nostrum adjutórium, fratrum nostrórum arbítrium consecrándos elégit, serváte in móribus vestris castæ, et sanctæ vitæ integritátem. Agnóscite, quod ágitis. Imitámini, quod tractátis; quátenus mortis Domínicæ mystérium celebrántes, mortificáre membra vestra a vítiis et concupiscéntiis ómnibus procurétis. Sit doctrína vestra spirituális medicína populo Dei. Sit odor vitæ vestræ delectaméntum Ecclésiæ Christi; ut prædicatióne, atque exémplo ædificétis domum, id est famíliam Dei; quátenus nec nos de vestra provectióne, nec vos de tanti offícii susceptióne damnári a Dómino sed remunerári pótius mereá-

but rather rewarded by the Lord. Which may he grant you, through his grace.

> After this all rise, and the **candidates** kneeling two by two successively before him, the Bishop standing before the faldstool with his mitre on, places both his hands on the head of each candidate successively, saying nothing. The new Priests, after the Bishop has imposed hands upon them, return and kneel before the altar. The Bishop, after he has imposed hands upon all the candidates, continues to stand, and holds his right hand extended and open toward them. All the Priests who are present, three or more of whom should be vested in chasubles, or at least stoles, if it be convenient, beginning at the Epistle side and walking in front of the candidates, who continue kneeling in a semicircle before the altar, place both their hands on each; then forming a semicircle, beginning at the Gospel side, they stand behind the candidates, holding their right hands extended toward them, after the manner of the Bishop. Then the Bishop, standing yet turned toward the candidates, says:

Let us, dearest brethren, beseech God the Father Almighty, to multiply his heavenly gifts on these his servants, whom he has chosen for the office of

mur. Quod ipse nobis concédat per grátiam suam. ℟. Amen.

Post hæc surgunt omnes, et ordinandis coram Pontifice binis et binis successive genuflectentibus, Pontifex stans ante faldistorium suum cum mitra, imponit simul utramque manum super caput cujuslibet ordinandi successive, nihil dicens. Novi Presbyteri, postquam Pontifex manus eis imposuit redeunt geniculatum ante altare. Pontifex posteaquam omnibus Ordinandis imposuit manus, prosequitur et manum dexteram extensam et apertam sustinet versus eosdem. Omnes sacerdotes qui adsunt, quorum tres, aut plures planetis vel saltem cum stolis parati, si commode fieri potest, esse debent, incipiendo a latere Epistolæ, et circumeuntes ante ordinandos in modum coronæ ante altare genuflexos, imponunt successive manum utramque super singulos genuflexos; deinde quemdam ferme semicirculum efficientes, incipiendo a latere Evangelii, consistunt a tergo ipsorum, sustinentes dexteram extensam versus eosdem quo modo suam sustinet Pontifex. Tunc Pontifex stans adhuc ad ordinandos conversus, dicit:

Orémus, fratres caríssimi, Deum Patrem omnipoténtem, ut super hos fámulos suos, quos ad Presbytérii munus elégit, cœléstia dona multí-

the Priesthood, and may what they receive through his mercy be ratified by his grace. Through Christ our Lord. Amen.

The Bishop, without his mitre, turned toward the altar, says:

Let us pray.

And the ministers:

Let us bend our knees.

℟. Rise up.

And then turned toward the candidates, says:

Hear us, we beseech thee, O Lord our God, and pour down upon these thy servants the blessing of the Holy Ghost, and the strength of priestly grace, that those whom in the sight of thy goodness we present for consecration, may be assisted by the unceasing bestowal of thy grace. Through our Lord Jesus Christ Thy Son, who liveth and reigneth with thee in the unity of the same Holy Ghost, God.

Then extending his hands before his breast, he says:

World without end.

℟. Amen.

plicet, et quod ejus dignatióne suscípiunt, ipsíus consequántur auxílio. Per Christum Dóminum nostrum. ℞. Amen.

Pontifex deposita mitra conversus ad altare, dicit:

Orémus.

Et ministri:

Flectámus génua.

℞. Leváte.

Et mox conversus ad ordinandos, dicit:

Exaudi nos, quæsumus Dómine Deus noster, et super hos fámulos tuos bene ✝ dictiónem Sancti Spíritus et grátiæ Sacerdotális infunde virtútem; ut quos tuæ pietátis aspéctibus offérimus consecrándos, perpétua múneris tui largitáte prosequáris. Per Dóminum nostrum Jesum Christum Fílium tuum, qui tecum vivit et regnat in unitáte ejúsdem Spíritus Sancti Deus.

Tum, extensis manibus ante pectus, dicit:

Per ómnia sæcula sæculórum.

℞. Amen.

V. The Lord be with you.

℟. And with thy spirit.

V. Lift up your hearts.

℟. We have lifted them up to the Lord.

V. Let us give thanks to the Lord our God.

℟. It is meet and just.

It is truly meet and right and profitable to salvation that we always and in all places give thanks to thee, O Holy Lord, Almighty Father, Eternal God, author of honors and distributor of all dignities, by whom all things advance, by whom all things are established, by whom the natural teachings of human understanding have been always expanded into that which is better, through the order arranged by thee with the perfection of reason. Wherefore the priestly dignity and the office of the Levites, instituted under typical forms, grew into something better; so, whilst thou didst appoint Pontiffs to be the supreme rulers of the people, thou didst choose for their associates and to

Dóminus vobíscum.

℞. Et cum spíritu tuo.

Sursum corda.

℞. Habémus ad Dóminum.

Grátias agámus Dómino Deo nostro.

℞. Dignum, et justum est.

Vere dignum, et justum est, æquum, et salutáre, nos tibi semper, et ubíque grátias ágere, Dómine sancte, Pater omnípotens, ætérne Deus, honórum auctor, et distribútor ómnium dignitátum; per quem profíciunt universa; per quem cuncta firmántur, amplificátis semper in mélius natúræ rationális increméntis, per órdinem cóngrua ratióne dispósitum. Unde et sacerdotáles gradus, atque officia Levitárum, Sacraméntis mysticis institúta crevérunt; ut cum Pontífices summos regéndis pópulis præfecísses, ad eórum societátis, et óperis adjuméntum, sequéntis órdinis viros, et secúndæ dig-

assist them in their work, men of an inferior order and a lower dignity. So in the desert thou didst breathe the spirit of Moses into the minds of seventy prudent men, with whose assistance he governed with ease countless multitudes of people, and so thou didst transfer to Eleazar and Ithamar, the sons of Aaron, of the abundance of their father's fullness, so that there might be sufficient priests for the saving sacrifices and more frequent sacraments. By this thy way, O Lord, thou didst give teachers of the faith as companions to the Apostles of Thy Son, by whose fruitful preaching they filled the whole world. Wherefore, we beseech thee, O Lord, grant to our infirmity also, those aids, forasmuch the weaker we are than they, by so much the more stand we in need of more helps. Bestow, we beseech thee, O Almighty Father, the dignity of the Priesthood upon these thy servants, renew in their breasts the spirit of sanctity, so that from thy hand, O

nitátis, elígeres. Sic in erémo per septuagínta virórum prudéntium mentes, Móysi spíritum propagásti, quibus ille adjutóribus usus, in pópulo innúmeras multitúdines fácile gubernávit. Sic et in Eleázarum, et Ithamárum fílios Aaron patérnæ plenitúdinis abundántiam transfudísti; ut ad hóstias salutáres, et frequentióris offícii Sacraménta ministérium suffíceret Sacerdótum. Hac providéntia, Dómine, Apóstolis fílii tui Doctóres fídei cómites addidísti, quibus illi orbem totum secúndis prædicatiónibus implevérunt. Quaprópter infirmitáti quoque nostræ, Dómine, quæsumus, hæc adjuménta largíre; qui quanto fragilióres sumus, tanto his plúribus indigémus. Da, quæsumus, omnípotens Pater, in hos fámulos tuos Presbytérii dignitátem, ínnova in viscéribus eórum Spíritum sanctitátis; ut accéptum a te, Deus, secúndi mériti munus obtíneant; cen-

God, they may receive this office, and make their lives worthy of imitation by others. May they be prudent fellow-workers of our order; may all the virtues shine in them, so that, being able to give a good account of the stewardship intrusted to them, they may obtain the rewards of eternal happiness.

What follows he reads in a low voice, in such a manner, however, that he can be heard by those standing near him.

Through the same Jesus Christ, thy Son, our Lord, who liveth and reigneth in the unity of the same Holy Ghost, God, world without end. Amen.

The Bishop sits with his mitre on, and adjusts the stole which each wears on his left shoulder: taking the part which hangs behind, and drawing it over the right shoulder, he arranges the stole before his breast in the form of a cross, saying to each:

Receive the yoke of the Lord, for his yoke is sweet and his burden light.

Afterwards he puts on each candidate successively the chasuble, the back part of which is folded and pinned up, saying to each:

Receive this priestly vestment, by

surámque morum exémplo suæ conversatiónis insínuent. Sint próvidi cooperatóres órdinis nostri; elúceat in eis totíus forma justítiæ, ut bonam ratiónem dispensatiónis sibi créditæ redditúri, ætérnæ beatitúdinis præmia consequántur.

Quod sequitur, legit submissa voce, ita tamen, quod a circumstantibus audiri possit.

Per eúmdem Dóminum nostrum Jesum Christum Fílium tuum, qui tecum vivit, et regnat in unitáte ejúsdem Spíritus sancti Deus, per ómnia sæcula sæculórum. ℞. Amen.

Pontifex sedet, accepta mitra, et reflectit stolam ab humero sinistro cujuslibet, capiens partem, quæ retro pendet, et imponens super dexterum humerum, aptat eam ante pectus, in modum crucis, singulis dicens :

Accipe jugum Dómini ; jugum enim ejus suáve est, et onus ejus leve.

Postea imponit cuilibet successive casulam, replicatam et convolutam acubus firmatam in parte posteriori, singulis dicens :

Accipe vestém sacerdotálem, per

which is signified charity; for God is powerful to increase charity in you, and make your works perfect.

The candidates answer:

Thanks be to God.

The Bishop rises without his mitre, all kneel, and he says:

O God, author of all holiness, whose consecration is true, and blessing bountiful; do thou, O Lord, pour down the gift of thy blessing upon these thy servants, whom we dedicate to the dignity of the Priesthood, so that by the gravity of their conduct and their manner of living they may show themselves elders, instructed by the teachings of Paul to Titus and Timothy, and thus meditating day and night upon thy Law, they may believe what they read, teach what they believe, practice what they teach. May they show forth in themselves justice, constancy, mercy, fortitude, and all the other virtues. May they incite others to the same by their example, confirm them by their admonitions, and preserve pure

quam cháritas intellígitur; potens est enim Deus, ut áugeat tibi charitátem, et opus perféctum.

Ordinandi respondent:

Deo Grátias.

Surgit Pontifex sine mitra, et omnibus genua flectentibus, dicit:

Deus sanctificatiónum ómnium auctor, cujus vera consecrátio, plénaque benedíctio est: tu, Dómine, super hos fámulos tuos, quos ad Presbytérii honórem dedicámus, munus tuæ bene ✝ dictiónis infúnde; ut gravitáte áctuum, et censúra vivendi probent se senióres, his institúti disciplínis, quas Tito, et Timótheo Paulus expósuit; ut in lege tua die ac nocte meditántes, quod légerint, credant; quod credíderint, dóceant; quod docúerint, imiténtur; justítiam constántiam, misericórdiam, fortitúdinem, cæterásque virtútes in se osténdant; exémplo præbeant, admonitióne confírment; ac purum et immaculátum ministérii sui donum custódiant;

and undefiled the gift of their ministry, and, for the benefit of thy people, may they change by an immaculate benediction the bread and wine into the Body and Blood of Thy Son. May they, by unspotted charity, grow up "unto a perfect man, unto the measure of the age of the fulness of Christ" (Eph. iv, 13), and rise on the day of the just and eternal judgment of God, with a pure conscience, true faith, and full of the Holy Ghost. Through the same Jesus Christ Thy Son, our Lord, who liveth and reigneth with thee in the unity of the same Holy Ghost, God, world without end. ℟. Amen.

Then the Bishop, without his mitre, turned towards the altar, kneels, and begins in a loud voice, and the choir continues the following hymn:

Come, O Creator, Spirit blest,
And in our souls take up thy rest;
Come, with thy grace and heavenly aid,
To fill the hearts which thou hast made.

The Bishop rises and proceeds with the ceremony of anointing the hands, as is described at the end

et in obséquium plebis tuæ, panem et vinum in Corpus et Sánguinem Fílii tui immaculáta benedictióne transfórment; et inviolábili charitáte in virum perféctum, in mensúram ætátis plenitúdinis Christi (Eph. iv, 13), in die justi, et ætérni judícii Dei consciéntia pura, fide vera, Spíritu Sancto pleni, resúrgant. Per eúmdem Dóminum nostrum Jesum Chrístum Fílium tuum, qui tecum vivit et regnat in unitáte ejúsdem Spíritus sancti Deus, per ómnia sæcula sæculórum. ℟. Amen.

Tunc Pontifex, sine mitra ante altare conversus, flexis genibus incipit alta voce, schola prosequente hymnum :

Veni, Creator Spiritus,
Mentes tuorum visita,
Imple superna gratia,
Quæ tu creasti pectora.

Hic Surgit Pontifex, et facit ut in fine hymni habetur: interim schola prosequitur hymnum ; qui

of the hymn, which the choir continues to sing, repeating it, except the first verse, if it be necessary on account of the number of the candidates.

Great Paraclete, to thee we cry,
O highest gift of God most high,
O fount of life, O fire of love,
And sweet anointing from above.

Thou in thy sevenfold gifts art known;
The finger of God's hand we own;
The promise of the Father thou,
Who dost the tongue with power endow.

Kindle our senses from above,
And make our hearts o'erflow with love;
With patience firm, and virtue high,
The weakness of our flesh supply.

Far from us drive the foe we dread,
And grant us thy true peace instead,
So shall we not, with thee for guide,
Turn from the path of life aside.

si propter Ordinandorum multitudinem necesse sit, repetatur, omisso primo versu :

Qui díceris Paráclitus,
Altíssimi donum Dei,
Fons vivus, ignis, cháritas,
Et spiritális únctio.

Tu septifórmis múnere,
Dígitus patérnæ déxteræ,
Tu rite promíssum Patris,
Sermóne dítans gúttura.

Accénde lumen sénsibus,
Infúnde amórem córdibus,
Infírma nostri córporis,
Virtúte firmans pérpeti.

Hostem repéllas lóngius,
Pacémque dones prótinus,
Ductóre sic te prævio,
Vitémus omne nóxium.

Oh may thy grace on us bestow,
The Father and the Son to know,
And Thee, through endless times confess'd,
Of both the Eternal Spirit bless'd.

To God the Father with the Son
And Holy Spirit, Three in One,
Be glory while the ages flow,
From all above and all below.
Amen.

(The hymn is thus concluded during the Octavo of Pentecost.)

All glory while the ages run,
Be to the Father and the Son
Who rose from death, the same to Thee,
O Holy Ghost, eternally.
Amen.

The first verse having been sung, the Bishop rises and sits with his mitre on, and the Candidates kneel before him successively; and the Bishop anoints with the oil of Catechumens, in the form of a cross both hands joined together, of each Candidate, forming with his right thumb dipped in the said oil two lines, namely from the thumb of the right hand to the index finger of the left, and from the thumb of the left hand to the index finger of the right, then anointing the entire palms, saying, while anointing each:

Per te sciámus da Patrem,
Noscámus atque Fílium,
Teque utriúsque Spíritum,
Credámus omni témpore.

Deo Patri sit glória,
Ejúsque soli Fílio,
Cum Spíritu Paráclito,
Nunc et per omne sæculum.
Amen.

(Tempore Paschali Hymnus terminandus est sic.)
Deo Patri sit glória,
Et Fílio qui a mórtuis,
Surréxit, ac Paráclito,
In sæculórum sæcula.
Amen.

Dicto primo Versu, surgit Pontifex et sedet cum mitra, et singuli Ordinandi successive coram eo genua flectunt; et Pontifex chm oleo catechumenorum inungit unicuique ambas manus simul junctas, in modum crucis, producendo cum pollice suo dextero in dictum oleum intincto duas lineas, videlicet, a pollice dextero manus usque ad indicem sinistræ, et a pollice sinistro usque ad indicem dexteræ, ungendo mox totaliter palmas, dicens, dum quemlibet inungit:

Vouchsafe, O Lord, to consecrate and sanctify these hands by this unction and our blessing. ℟. Amen.

The Bishop makes with his right hand the sign of the cross over the hands of each whom he ordains, and continues:

That whatever they shall bless may be blessed and whatever they shall consecrate may be consecrated and sanctified in the name of our Lord Jesus Christ.

And each of those ordained answers:

Amen.

Then the Bishop closes the hands of each successively, which, thus consecrated, one of the ministers binds with a white linen cloth, putting the right hand on the left; and then each returns to his place in the ranks, and holds his hands thus closed and bound. When the hands of all have been anointed and consecrated, the Bishop rubs his thumb with a small piece of bread; then he presents to each successively a chalice containing wine and water, and a paten upon it, with a host, and they touch at the same time the host and the paten and the cup of the chalice, while the Bishop says to each:

Receive power to offer sacrifice, and

Consecráre, et sanctificáre dignéris, Dómine, manus istas per istam unctiónem, et nostram bene✝dictiónem. ℟. Amen.

Pontifex producit manu dextera signum crucis super manus illius quem ordinat, et prosequitur,

Ut quæcúmque benedíxerint, benedicántur, et quæcúmque consecráverint, consecréntur, et sanctificéntur, in nómine Dómini nostri Jesu Christi.

Et quilibet ordinandus respondet :
Amen.

Tum Pontifex claudit, manus cujuslibet successive, quas sic consecratas aliquis ministrorum Pontificis albo panniculo lineo simul, videlicet, dexteram super sinistram alligat, et mox unusquisque ad ordinem suum redit; et sic clausas, et alligatas manus tenet. Omnium manibus unctis, et consecratis, Pontifex pollicem mica panis tergit; tum tradit cuilibet successive Calicem cum vino, et aqua, et Patenam superpositam cum Hostia et ipsi Hostiam, et Patenam et cuppam Calicis simul tangunt, Pontifice singulis dicente :

Accipe potestátem offérre sacrifícium

to celebrate Masses, both for the living and for the dead. ℞. Amen.

After the newly Ordained have touched the chalice and the paten, they go to the sacristy and there wash their hands, and return to the places which they occupied upon entering the church. The Mass proceeds as usual to the Offertory inclusively.

At the proper time one of the newly ordained Deacons goes to the gospel side, and reads the gospel at the same time with the Bishop.

The Bishop, after having read the Offertory, puts on his mitre, goes to the faldstool before the middle of the altar, and there receives the offering from all those ordained: all of whom go up two by two to the Bishop, and kneeling offer him each a lighted candle and kiss his hand: first the Priests. then the Deacons successively and the others according to order.

After this the Bishop continues Mass. All those ordained return to their places except the new priests, who, arranged behind the Bishop in a semicircle, or here and there as found most convenient, kneeling on the floor, have their Missals before them, and recite, together with the Bishop, the remaining portion of the Mass, namely:

The Offertory.

Accept, O holy Father, almighty and eternal God, this unspotted Host,

Deo, missásque celebráre, tam pro vivis, quam pro defúnctis. In nómine Dómini. ℞. Amen.

Postquam Ordinati tetigerunt Calicem et Patenam accedunt ad Sacristiam, ibique manus suas lavant, et redeunt ad loca quæ Ecclesiam ingressi occupabant. Proceditur in Missa ordine solito usque ad Offertorium inclusive.

Tempore opportuno unus ex Diaconis noviter Ordinatis accedit ad latus Evangelii et simul cum Pontifice Evangelium legit.

Pontifex vero, Offertorio lecto, accepta mitra, vadit ad faldistorium ante medium altaris, et ibi sedens accipit offertorium ab omnibus Ordinatis, qui omnes accedunt, bini et bini, ad Pontificem, coram quo genuflexi offerunt illi singulas candelas accensas, et osculantur ejus manum; primo Presbyteri tum Diaconi successive, et alii suo ordine.

Post hæc Pontifex prosequitur Missam. Omnes Ordinati, exceptis Novis Presbyteris, redeunt ad loca sua. Presbyteri vero post Pontificem in modum coronæ ordinati vel hinc et inde, ubi magis commodum est, in terra genuflexi habent Missalia coram se, et recitant simul cum Pontifice omnia alia de Missa, videlicet:

Offertorium.

Súscipe, sancte Pater omnípotens ætérne Deus, hanc immaculátam Hós-

which I thy unworthy servant offer unto thee, my living and true God, for my innumerable sins, offences, and negligences, and for all here present; as also for all faithful Christians, both living and dead; that it may avail me and them unto salvation, and life everlasting. Amen.

Then they continue with the Bishop, who says:

O God! who in creating human nature, didst wonderfully dignify it, and who didst still more wonderfully reform it; grant that by the mystery of this water and wine, we may be made partakers of his divinity, who vouchsafed to become partaker of our humanity, Jesus Christ, thy Son, our Lord; who with thee and the Holy Ghost, liveth and reigneth one God, for ever and ever. Amen.

While the Bishop offers the Chalice they say with him:

We offer unto thee, O Lord, the chalice of salvation, beseeching thy

tiam, quam ego indígnus fámulus tuus offéro tibi, Deo meo, vivo et vero, pro innumerabílibus peccátis, et offensiónibus, et negligéntiis meis, et pro ómnibus circumstántibus, sed et pro ómnibus fidélibus Christiánis vivis, atque defúnctis: ut mihi, et illis profíciat ad salútem in vitam æternam. Amen.

Deinde prosequuntur cum Pontifice dicente:

Deus qui humánæ substántiæ dignitátem mirabíliter condidísti, et mirabílius reformásti; da nobis per hujus aquæ et vini mystérium, ejus divinitátis esse consórtes, qui humanitátis nostræ fíeri dignátus est párticeps, Jesus Christus fílius tuus Dóminus noster: qui tecum vivit, et regnat in unitáte Spíritus sancti Deus: per ómnia sæcula sæculórum. Amen.

Dum Pontifex offert Calicem, cum eo dicunt:

Offerimus tibi Dómine, Cálicem salutáris, tuam deprecántes cleméntiam:

clemency: that it may ascend before thy divine Majesty, as a sweet odor, for our salvation, and for that of the whole world. Amen.

Then they continue:

In a spirit of humility and with contrition of heart, we pray thee, O Lord, to make us acceptable to thee; and let our sacrifice be so performed this day, in thy sight, that it may be pleasing to thee, O Lord our God.

Come, O almighty and eternal God, the sanctifier, and bless this sacrifice, prepared for the glory of thy holy name.

While the Bishop washes his hands.

I will wash my hands among the innocent: and will compass thy altar, O Lord. That I may hear the voice of thy praise, and tell all thy wondrous works.

I have loved, O Lord, the beauty of thy house, and the place where thy glory dwelleth.

Take not away my soul, O God!

ut in conspéctu divínæ Majestátis tuæ pro nostra, et totíus mundi salúte cum odóre suavitátis ascéndat. Amen.

Deinde prosequuntur:
In spíritu humilitátis, et in ánimo contríto suscipiámur a te, Dómine, et sic fiat sacrifícium nostrum in conspéctu tuo hódie ut pláceat tibi, Dómine Deus.

Veni sanctificátor omnípotens ætérne Deus: et bénedic hoc sacrifícium, tuo sancto nómini præparátum.

Dum Pontifex lavat manus.
Lavabo inter innocéntes manus meas, et circúmdabo altáre tuum, Dómine. Ut áudiam vocem laudis: et enárrem univérsa mirabília tua.

Dómine diléxi decórem domus tuæ, et locum habitatiónis glóriæ tuæ.
Ne perdas cum ímpiis, Deus, ánimam

with the wicked; nor my life with bloody men.

In whose hands are iniquities: their right hand is filled with gifts.

But I have walked in my innocence; redeem me and have mercy on me. My foot hath stood in the direct way: in the churches I will bless thee, O Lord.

Glory be to the Father, and the Son, and the Holy Ghost. As it was in the beginning now and ever shall be, world without end. Amen.

The Bishop being inclined in the middle of the altar they say with him:

Receive, O holy Trinity, this oblation which we make to thee in memory of the Passion, Resurrection, and Ascension of our Lord Jesus Christ, and in honor of the blessed Mary, ever Virgin, of blessed John Baptist, of the holy Apostles Peter and Paul, of these and of all the saints; that it may avail to their honor, and to our salvation; and may they vouchsafe to intercede for

meam, et cum viris sánguinum vitam meam.

In quorum mánibus iniquitátes sunt, déxtera eórum repléta est munéribus.

Ego autem in innocéntia mea ingréssus sum: rédime me, et miserére mei. Pes meus stetit in dirécto: in Ecclésiis benedícam te, Dómine.

Glória Patri, et Fílio, et Spirítui sancto. Sicut erat in princípio, et nunc, et semper et in sæcula sæculórum. Amen.

Pontifice in medio altaris inclinato, cum ipso dicunt:

Súscipe, sancta Trínitas, hanc oblatiónem, quam tibi offérimus ob memóriam passiónis, resurrectiónis, et ascensiónis Jesu Christi Dómini nostri: et in honóre Beátæ Maríæ semper Vírginis, et Beáti Joánnis Baptístæ, et Sanctórum Apostolórum Petri, et Pauli, et istórum, et ómnium Sanctórum: ut illis profíciat ad honórem,

us in heaven, whose memory we celebrate on earth. Through the same Christ our Lord. Amen.

Then they say with the Bishop:

Brethren, pray that my sacrifice and yours may be acceptable to God, the Father Almighty.

When the ministers have responded,

May the Lord receive, etc.,

Those ordained say,

Amen.

Then they say the secrets.

Secret.*

Hear us, O Lord, we beseech thee, and, being appeased by these offerings, grant they may increase our devotion and advance our salvation.

For those Ordained.

Enable us, by thy mysteries, we be-

---

* The Secrets, Preface, Communion, and Post Communions are given for the Saturday of the Ember days of Advent. They vary for the different seasons at which Ordinations take place.

nobis autem ad salútem, et illi pro nobis intercédere dignéntur in cœlis, quorum memóriam ágimus in terris. Per eúmdem Christum Dóminum nostrum. Amen.

Deinde dicunt cum Pontifice ;

Orate, Fratres: ut meum ac vestrum sacrifícium acceptábile fiat apud Deum Patrem omnipoténtem,

Dum ministri responderint,

Suscípiat, etc.,

Ordinati dicunt,

Amen.

Deinde dicunt orationes secretas.

Secreta.*

Sacrificiis præséntibus, quæsumus Dómine, placátus inténde: ut et devotióni nostræ profíciant, et salúti.

Pro Ordinatis :

Tuis, quæsumus Dómine, operáre

---

* Secretæ, Præfatio, Communio et Post Communio Sabbati Quatuor Temporum Adventus hic indicantur. Mutantur autem iuxta varia tempora quibus Ordinationes fiunt

seech thee, O Lord, to offer with worthy souls, these gifts to thee. Through our Lord Jesus Christ Thy Son, who with thee and the Holy Ghost liveth and reigneth one God, forever and ever. Amen.

The Other Secrets.
Of the B. V. M.

Strengthen, we beseech thee, O Lord, in our souls, the mysteries of the true faith, that we who confess him, that was conceived of a virgin, to be true God and true man, may, by the power of his saving resurrection deserve to come to eternal joys.

Against the Persecutors of the Church,

Protect us, O Lord, while we assist at thy sacred mysteries, that being employed in acts of religion, we may serve thee both in body and mind. Through our Lord Jesus Christ, Thy Son, who with thee and the Holy Ghost liveth and reigneth one God, forever and ever. Amen.

mystériis: ut hæc tibi múnera dignis méntibus offerámus. Per Dóminum nostrum Jesum Christum Fílium tuum; qui tecum vivit, et regnat in unitáte Spíritus sancti Deus; per ómnia sæcula sæculórum. Amen.

Aliæ Secretæ.
De Sancta Maria.

In méntibus nostris, quæsumus Dómine, veræ fídei Sacraménta confírma; ut, qui concéptum de Vírgine Deum verum et hóminem confitémur; per ejus salutíferæ resurrectiónis poténtiam, ad ætérnam mereámur perveníre lætítiam.

Contra Persecutores Ecclesiæ:

Protege nos, Dómine, tuis mystériis serviéntes: ut divínis rebus inhæréntes, et córpore tibi famulémur et mente. Per Dóminum nostrum Jesum Christum Fílium tuum: qui tecum vivit, et regnat in unitáte Spíritus sancti Deus: per ómnia sæcula sæculórum,

Or for the Pope.

Be appeased, O Lord, with the offering we have made, and cease not to protect thy servant N., whom thou hast been pleased to appoint Pastor over thy Church. Through our Lord Jesus Christ Thy Son, who with thee and the Holy Ghost liveth and reigneth one God

V. World without end.

℞. Amen.

V. The Lord be with you.

℞. And with thy spirit.

V. Lift up your hearts.

℞. We have lifted them up to the Lord.

V. Let us give thanks to the Lord our God.

℞. It is meet and just.

Preface.*

It is truly meet and just, right and available to salvation, that we should always, and in all places, give thanks to thee, O holy Lord, Father Al-

---

* See note, page 77.

Vel Pro Papa:

Oblatis, quæsumus Dómine, placáre munéribus: et fámulum tuum N., quem Pastórem Ecclésiæ tuæ præésse voluísti, assídua protectióne gubérna. Per Dóminum nostrum Jesum Christum Fílium tuum: qui tecum vivit et regnat in unitáte Spíritus Sancti Deus

Per ómnia sæcula sæculórum.

℟. Amen.

V. Dóminus vobíscum.

℟. Et cum spíritu tuo.

V. Sursum corda.

℟. Habémus ad Dóminum.

V. Grátias agámus Dómino Deo nostro.

℟. Dignum et justum est.

Præfatio.*

Vere dignum, et justum est, æquum et salutáre, nos tibi semper, et ubíque grátias ágere: Dómine Sancte, Pater omnípotens, ætérne Deus: per Chris-

---

* Vide not., pag. 77.

mighty, eternal God. Through Christ our Lord: by whom the angels praise thy majesty, the dominations adore it, the powers tremble before it, the heavens, the heavenly virtues, and blessed seraphim, with common jubilee glorify it. Together with whom we beseech thee, that we may be admitted to join our humble voices, saying: Holy, holy, holy, Lord God of Sabaoth, Heaven and earth are full of thy glory, Hosanna in the highest. Blessed is he that cometh in the name of the Lord, Hosanna in the highest.

Then the Canon is begun.

THE CANON OF THE MASS.

We therefore humbly pray and beseech thee, most merciful Father, through Jesus Christ thy Son, our Lord, that thou wouldst accept and bless these gifts, these presents, these holy unspotted sacrifices which, in the first place, we offer to thee for thy holy Catholic Church, to which vouchsafe to grant peace; preserve,

tum Dóminum nostrum. Per quem Majestátem tuam laudant Angeli, adórant Dominatiónes, tremunt Potestátes. Cœli Cœlorúmque Virtútes, ac beáta Séraphim, sócia exultatióne concélebrant. Cum quibus et nostras voces, ut admítti júbeas, deprecámur, súpplici confessióne dicéntes: Sanctus, Sanctus, Sanctus, Dóminus Deus Sábaoth. Pleni sunt cœli, et terra glória tua. Hosánna in excélsis. Benedíctus qui venit in nómine Dómini. Hosánna in excélsis.

Deinde incipitur Canon:

CANON MISSÆ.

Te ígitur, clementíssime Pater, per Jesum Christum fílium tuum, Dóminum nostrum, súpplices rogámus ac pétimus,—uti accépta hábeas, et benedícas hæc—dona, hæc—múnera, hæc—sancta sacrifícia illibáta, imprímis quæ tibi offérimus pro Ecclésia tua sancta cathólica, quam pacificáre, custodíre,

unite, and govern it throughout the world; together with thy servant our Pope N., our Bishop N.

While the Bishop says, "And with thy unworthy servant," they say, "And with our Bishop N.," expressing the name of the Bishop who is the Ordinary of the place where they are ordained, even if the consecrator be his suffragan or from another diocese.

And all orthodox believers and professors of the Catholic and Apostolic faith.

Commemoration of the Living.

Be mindful, O Lord, of thy servants, men and women, N. and N.

They join their hands and pray for a little while for those for whom they intend to pray; then they continue with the Bishop:

And of all here present, whose faith and devotion are known to thee, for whom we offer; or who offer up to thee this sacrifice of praise for themselves, and all that are dear to them; for the redemption of their souls, for the health and salvation they hope for, and for which they now pay their vows to thee, the eternal, living, and true God.

RITUS ORDINATIONIS. 81

adunáre et régere dignéris toto orbe terrárum; una, cum fámulo tuo Papa nostro N. et Antístite nostro N.

Dum Pontifex dicit, "Et me indigno servo tuo," ipsi dicunt "Et Antistite nostro N." exprimendo nomen Episcopi, qui est Ordinarius loci ubi consecrantur, etiam si consecrans sit ejus suffraganeus aut extraneus.

Et ómnibus orthodóxis, atque Cathólicæ et Apostólicæ fídei cultóribus:

Commemoratio Pro Vivis.

Memento Dómine, famulórum, famularúmque tuárum, N. and N.

Jungunt manus, orant aliquantulum pro quibus orare intendunt; deinde, cum Pontifice prosequuntur:

Et ómnium circumstántium, quorum tibi fides cógnita est, et nota devótio, pro quibus tibi offérimus: vel qui tibi ófferunt hoc Sacrifícium laudis, pro se, suísque ómnibus: pro redemptióne animárum suárum, pro spe salútis, et incolumitátis suæ: tibíque reddunt vota sua ætérno Deo, vivo et vero.

* Communicating with and honoring in the first place the memory of the ever glorious Virgin Mary, Mother of our God and Lord Jesus Christ; as also of the blessed Apostles and Martyrs, Peter and Paul, Andrew, James, John, Thomas, James, Philip, Bartholomew, Matthew, Simon and Thaddeus, Linus, Cletus, Clement, Xystus, Cornelius, Cyprian, Lawrence, Chrysogonus, John and Paul, Cosmas and Damian, and of all thy Saints; by whose merits and prayers grant that we may be always defended by the help of thy protection. Through the same Christ our Lord. Amen.

We therefore beseech thee, O Lord, graciously to accept this oblation of our servitude, which is also that of thy whole family; dispose our days in thy peace, preserve us from eternal damnation, and place us in the number of thine

---

* On Holy Saturday, and the Saturday within the Octave of Pentecost, in place of the following prayers two others are said.

* Communicantes, et memóriam venerántes, in primis gloriósæ semper Vírginis Maríæ, genitrícis Dei et Dómini nostri Jesu Christi : sed et beatórum Apostolórum, ac Mártyrum tuórum, Petri et Pauli, Andréæ, Jacóbi, Joánnis, Thomæ, Jacóbi, Philíppi, Bartholómæi, Matthæi, Simónis, et Thaddæi: Lini, Cleti, Cleméntis, Xysti, Cornélii, Cypriáni, Lauréntii, Chrysógoni, Joánnis et Pauli, Cosmæ et Damiáni ; et ómnium Sanctórum tuórum : quorum méritis precibúsque concédas, ut in ómnibus protectiónis tuæ muniámur auxílio. Per eúmdem Christum Dóminum nostrum. Amen.

Hanc ígitur oblatiónem servitútis nostræ, sed et cunctæ famíliæ tuæ; quæsumus Dómine, ut placátus accípias; díesque nostros in tua pace dispónas, atque ab ætérna damnatióne

---

* Sabbato Sancto, et Sabbato Pentecostes pro sequentibus orationibus duæ aliæ substituuntur.

elect. Through Christ our Lord. Amen.

Vouchsafe, we beseech thee, O God! to make this oblation in all things blessed, approved, ratified, reasonable, and acceptable; that it may be made for us the body and blood of thy most beloved Son Jesus Christ our Lord.

Who the day before he suffered, took bread into his holy and venerable hands, and with his eyes lifted up towards heaven, to thee, O God! his Almighty Father, giving thee thanks; he blessed it, broke it, and gave it to his disciples, saying: Take and eat ye all of this:

Then they pronounce the words of consecration, distinctly and attentively, at the same moment that they are said by the Bishop:

FOR THIS IS MY BODY.

Having adored the Host by an inclination of the head, they say:

nos éripi, et in electórum tuórum júbeas grege numerári. Per Christum Dóminum nostrum. Amen.

Quam oblatiónem tu Deus in ómnibus, quæsumus bene—díctam, adscrí—ptam, ra—tam, rationábilem, acceptabilémque fácere dignéris: ut nobis Cor—pus et San—guis fiat dilectíssimi fílii tui Dómini nostri Jesu Christi.

Qui prídie quam paterétur, accépit panem in sanctas ac venerábiles manus suas: et elevátis óculis in cœlum ad te Deum Patrem suum omnipoténtem, tibi grátias agens, bene—díxit, fregit dedítque Discípulis suis dicens: Accípite, et manducáte ex hoc omnes:

Deinde proferunt verba consecrationis, distincte et attente, eodem momento quo dicuntur ab Episcopo.

HOC EST ENIM CORPUS MEUM.

Adorata hostia capitis inclinatione, dicunt:

In like manner, after he had supped, taking also this excellent chalice into his holy and venerable hands, again giving thee thanks, he blessed it, and gave it to his disciples, saying: Take and drink ye all of this.

Then they pronounce the words of consecration of the chalice:

FOR THIS IS THE CHALICE OF MY BLOOD OF THE NEW AND EVERLASTING TESTAMENT: A MYSTERY OF FAITH: WHICH SHALL BE SHED FOR YOU, AND FOR MANY, TO THE REMISSION OF SINS.

As often as you do these things, ye shall do them in remembrance of me.

Then they continue with the Bishop:

Wherefore, O Lord, we thy servants, as also thy holy people, being mindful of the blessed passion of the same Christ thy Son our Lord, and of his resurrection from hell, as also of his glorious ascension into heaven, offer to thy most excellent Majesty of thy own gifts and

Simili modo postquam cœnátum est accípiens et hunc præclárum Cálicem in sanctas ac venerábiles manus suas: item tibi grátias agens, bene—díxit, dedítque Discípulis suis, dicens: accípite, et bíbite ex eo omnes.

Deinde proferunt verba Consecrationis Calicis :

HIC EST ENIM CALIX SANGUINIS MEI, NOVI ET ÆTERNI TESTAMENTI: MYSTERIUM FIDEI: QUI PRO VOBIS ET PRO MULTIS EFFUNDETUR IN REMISSIONEM PECCATORUM.

Hæc quotiescúmque fecéritis, in mei memóriam faciétis.

Deinde cum Pontifice prosequuntur :

Unde et mémores, Dómine, nos servi tui, sed et plebs tua sancta, ejúsdem Christi fílii tui Dómini nostri, tam beátæ passiónis, nec non et ab ínferis resurrectiónis, sed et in cœlos gloriósæ ascensiónis, offérimus præcláræ majes-

favors, a pure Host, a holy Host, an unspotted Host, the holy bread of eternal life, and chalice of everlasting salvation.

Upon which vouchsafe to look, with a propitious and serene countenance, and to accept them, as thou wert pleased to accept the gifts of thy just servant Abel, and the sacrifice of our Patriarch Abraham, and that which thy High Priest Melchisedech offered to thee, a holy sacrifice, and unspotted victim.

We humbly beseech thee, O Almighty God, command these to be carried by the hands of thy holy angels to thy altar above, in the sight of thy divine Majesty, that as many as shall partake of the most sacred body and blood of thy Son at this altar, may be filled with every heavenly blessing and grace. Through the same Christ our Lord. Amen.

Commemoration of the Dead.

táti tuæ de tuis donis ac datis, hóstiam —puram, hóstiam—sanctam, hóstiam—immaculátam, panem—sanctum vitæ ætérnæ, et Cálicem—salútis perpétuæ.

Supra quæ propítio, ac seréno vultu respícere dignéris: et accépta habére, sícuti accépta habére dignátus es múnera púeri tui justi Abel, et sacrifícium Patriárchæ nostri Abrahæ; et quod tibi óbtulit summus Sacérdos tuus Melchísedech, sanctum sacrifícium, immaculátam hóstiam.

Supplices te rogámus omnípotens Deus: jube hæc perférri per manus sancti Angeli tui in sublíme altáre tuum, in conspéctu divínæ Majestátis tuæ: ut quotquot,—ex hac altáris participatióne, sacrosánctum Fílii tui Corpus et Sánguinem sumpsérimus, omni benedictióne cœlésti, et grátia repleámur. Per eúmdem Christum Dóminum nostrum. Amen.

Commemoratio pro Defunctis.

Remember, O Lord, also thy servants, men and women, N. and N., who are gone before us with the sign of Faith, and repose in the sleep of peace.

They join their hands and pray a little while for those for whom they intend to pray; then they continue with the Bishop:

To these, O Lord, and to all that rest in Christ, grant, we beseech thee, a place of refreshment, light, and peace; through the same Christ our Lord. Amen.

They strike their breasts with their right hands, saying:

To us sinners also, thy servants, hoping in the multitude of thy mercies, vouchsafe to grant some part and fellowship with thy holy apostles and martyrs; with John, Stephen, Matthias, Barnaby, Ignatius, Alexander, Marcellinus, Peter, Felicitas, Perpetua, Agatha, Lucy, Agnes, Cecilia, Anastasia, and with all thy saints; into whose company we beseech thee to admit us, not in consideration of our merits,

Memento étiam, Dómine, famulórum famularúmque tuárum, N. et N., qui nos præcessérunt cum signo fídei, et dórmiunt in somno pacis.

Jungunt manus, orant aliquantulum pro quibus orare intendunt; deinde cum Pontifice prosequuntur:

Ipsis, Dómine, et ómnibus in Christo quiescéntibus, locum refrigérii, lucis et pacis, ut indúlgeas, deprecámur. Per eúmdem Christum Dóminum nostrum. Amen.

Manu dextera percutiunt pectus, dicentes:

Nobis quoque peccatóribus fámulis tuis, de multitúdine miseratiónum tuárum sperántibus, partem áliquam et societátem donáre dignéris, cum tuis sanctis Apóstolis et Martyribus: cum Joánne, Stéphano, Mathía, Bárnaba, Ignátio, Alexándro, Marcellíno, Petro, Felicitáte, Perpétua, Agatha, Lúcia, Agnéte, Cæcília, Anastásia, et ómnibus Sanctis tuis: intra quorum nos consór-

but of thy own gratuitous favor. Through Christ our Lord.

By whom, O Lord, thou dost always create, sanctify, quicken, bless, and give us all these good things.

HERE A SHORT PAUSE IS MADE.

By him, and with him, and in him, is to thee, God the Father Almighty, in the unity of the Holy Ghost all honor and glory.

World without end.

Let us pray. Instructed by thy saving precepts, and following thy divine directions, we presume to say: Our Father, who art in heaven, hallowed be thy name; thy kingdom come; thy will be done on earth as it is in heaven. Give us this day our daily bread; and forgive us our trespasses, as we forgive them that trespass against us. And lead us not into temptation.

tium, non æstimátor mériti, sed véniæ, quæsumus, largítor admítte. Per Christum Dóminum nostrum.

Per quem hæc ómnia, Dómine, semper bona creas, sanctí—ficas, viví—ficas, bene—dícis, et præstas nobis.

PAUSATUR HIC ALIQUANTULUM.

Per ip-sum, et cum ip-so, et in ip-so, est tibi Deo Patri—omnipoténti, in unitáte Spíritus—sancti, omnis honor et glória.

Per ómnia sæcula sæculórum.

Orémus. Præcéptis salutáribus móniti, et divína institutióne formáti, audémus dícere : Pater noster, qui es in cœlis : Sanctificétur nomen tuum : Advéniat regnum tuum. Fiat volúntas tua, sicut in cœlo, et in terra : Panem nostrum quotidiánum da nobis hódie ; Et dimítte nobis débita nostra, sicut et nos dimíttimus debitóribus nostris : Et ne nos indúcas in tentatiónem.

After, But deliver us from evil, they say:

Amen. Deliver us, we beseech thee, O Lord! from all evils, past, present, and to come; and by the intercession of the blessed and glorious ever Virgin Mary, Mother of God, and of thy blessed Apostles Peter and Paul, and of Andrew, and of all the saints, mercifully grant peace in our days; that by the assistance of thy mercy we may be always free from sin and secure from all disturbance.

Here a short pause is made.

Through the same Jesus Christ our Lord thy Son, who with thee and the Holy Ghost, liveth and reigneth one God, world without end.

The peace of the Lord be always with you.

After the ministers have answered, *And with thy spirit*, they say:

May this mixture and consecration of the body and blood of our Lord

Post, *Sed líbera nos a malo*, dicunt :

Amen. Líbera nos, quæsumus Dómine, ab ómnibus malis prætéritis, præséntibus, et futuris : et intercedénte beáta et gloriósa semper Vírgine Dei genitríce María, cum beatis Apóstolis tuis Petro et Paulo, atque Andréa, et ómnibus Sanctis, da propítius pacem in diébus nostris : ut ope misericórdiæ tuæ adjúti, et a peccáto simus semper líberi, et ab omni perturbatióne secúri.

Pausatur hic aliquantulum.

Per eúmdem Dóminum nostrum Jesum Christum Fílium tuum, qui tecum vivit et regnat in unitáte Spíritus sancti Deus. Per ómnia sæcula sæculórum.

Pax—Dómini sit—semper vobís—cum.

Postquam a ministris responsum fuerit, *Et cum spiritu tuo*, dicunt :

Hæc commíxtio, et consecrátio Córporis et Sánguinis Dómini nostri Jesu

Jesus Christ, be to us that receive them effectual to eternal life. Amen.

Then striking their breasts three times, they say:

Lamb of God, who takest away the sins of the world, have mercy upon us.

Lamb of God, who takest away the sins of the world, have mercy upon us.

Lamb of God, who takest away the sins of the world, give us peace.

Lord Jesus Christ, who didst say to thy apostles, I leave you peace, I give you my peace, look not upon my sins, but on the faith of thy church; and vouchsafe to grant it that peace and union which is according to thy will: who livest and reignest, God, for ever and ever. Amen.

Here the Bishop rises, kisses the altar and gives the Pax to the first of those Ordained to each Holy Order, who come up one after another, and before receiving it kiss the altar at the right of the Bishop, who says:

Peace be with thee.

And each one answers:

And with thy spirit.

Christi, fiat accipiéntibus nobis in vitam ætérnam. Amen.

<small>Dein ter pectus percutientes, dicunt :</small>

Agnus Dei, qui tollis peccáta mundi, miserére nobis.

Agnus Dei, qui tollis peccáta mundi, miserére nobis.

Agnus Dei, qui tollis peccáta mundi, dona nobis pacem.

Domine Jesu Christe, qui dixísti Apóstolis tuis : Pacem relínquo vobis, pacem meam do vobis ; ne respícias peccáta mea, sed fidem Ecclésiæ tuæ : eámque secúndum voluntátem tuam pacificáre, et coadunáre dignéris. Qui vivis et regnas Deus, per ómnia sæcula sæculórum. Amen.

<small>Hic Pontifex osculatur altare et dat primo ex singulis Ordinatis cujuslibet Ordinis sacri ad eum successive accedenti, et altare prius ad dexteram Pontificis deosculanti, pacem, dicens :</small>

Pax tecum.

<small>Cui ille respondet :</small>

Et cum spíritu tuo.

And each of them gives the *Pax* to the one next ordained to the same Order with him, and this one to the next, and so on to the end. But if the number of Candidates be small the Bishop gives the *Pax* to each. The last of the Subdeacons gives the *Pax* to the first of the Acolytes ordained, and he gives it to the others who have received Minor Orders and Tonsure.

Afterwards the Bishop continues the Mass, together with the New Priests.

Lord Jesus Christ, Son of the living God, who, according to the will of the Father, and by the co-operation of the Holy Ghost, hast through thy death given life to the world, deliver me by this thy most sacred Body and Blood from all my iniquities, and from all evils; and make me always adhere to thy commandments, and never suffer me to be separated from thee; who with the same God the Father and the Holy Ghost, liveth and reigneth, God, for ever and ever. Amen.

Let not the participation of thy body, O Lord Jesus Christ! which, though unworthy, I presume to receive, turn to my judgment and condemna-

Et quilibet illorum dat sequenti sui ordinis secum ordinato et ille alteri, et sic usque ad ultimum continuatur. Si autem Ordinatorum parvus sit numerus, Pontifex dat pacem singulis. Ultimus Subdiaconus pacem dat primo Acolytho ordinato, et hic eam communicat reliquis promotis ad ordines minores et ad tonsuram.

Postea Pontifex prosequitur Missam una cum Novis Presbyteris.

Domine Jesu Christe, Fili Dei vivi, qui ex voluntáte Patris, co-operánte Spíritu sancto, per mortem tuam mundum vivificásti: líbera me per hoc sacrosánctum Corpus, et Sánguinem tuum, ab ómnibus iniquitátibus meis, et univérsis malis; et fac me tuis semper inhærére mandátis, et a te nunquam separári permíttas: qui cum eódem Deo Patre et Spíritu sancto, vivis et regnas Deus in sæcula sæculórum. Amen.

Perceptio Córporis tui, Dómine Jesu Christe, quod ego indígnus súmere præsúmo, non mihi provéniat in judícium, et condemnatiónem: sed pro tua

tion, but through thy mercy, let it be for me a safeguard and remedy, of soul and body; who with God the Father, and the Holy Ghost, livest and reignest one God, for ever and ever. Amen.

I will take the heavenly bread, and invoke the name of the Lord.

Then placing their left hands on their breasts they strike their breasts three times, and say thrice, devoutly and humbly with the Bishop:

Lord, I am not worthy that thou shouldst enter under my roof; but only say the word, and my soul shall be healed.

Then they continue with the Bishop:

The body of our Lord Jesus Christ preserve my soul to life everlasting. Amen.

After a short meditation they say with the Bishop:

What return shall I make to the Lord for all that he has given me?

HERE A SHORT PAUSE IS MADE.

I will take the Chalice of salvation, and call upon the name of the Lord. Praising, I will call upon the Lord, and I shall be safe from my enemies.

pietáte, prosit mihi ad tutaméntum mentis et córporis, et ad medélam percipiéndam. Qui vivis et regnas cum Deo Patre, in unitáte Spíritus sancti Deus, per ómnia sæcula sæculórum. Amen.

Panem cœléstem accípiam, et nomen Dómini invocábo.

Tum manum sinistram ponentes infra pectus, dextera ter illud percutiunt, et dicunt ter devote et humiliter cum Pontifice.

Domine, non sum dignus, ut intres sub tectum meum: sed tantum dic verbo et sanábitur ánima mea.

Tum prosequuntur cum Pontifice:

Corpus Dómini nostri Jesu Christi custódiat ánimam meam in vitam ætérnam. Amen.

Post meditationem parvam dicunt cum Pontifice:

Quid retríbuam Dómino pro ómnibus quæ retríbuit mihi?

PAUSATUR HIC ALIQUANTULUM.

Cálicem salutáris accípiam, et nomen Dómini invocábo. Laudans invocábo Dóminum, et ab inimícis meis salvus ero.

The blood of our Lord Jesus Christ preserve my soul to everlasting life. Amen.

After the Bishop has communicated, those ordained to the Priesthood rise and go to the altar, and the Bishop gives them communion, using this form:

The Body of our Lord Jesus Christ preserve thee to life everlasting.

Each one answers, *Amen*, kisses the hand of the Bishop, and receives the Sacred Particle.

Afterwards, the rest of those ordained, kneeling before the altar, recite the *Confiteor* in a low voice, after which the Bishop says, as usual, "May Almighty God," &c., and "May the Almighty and merciful Lord," &c., and gives them communion, using the same form as for the priests.

One of the ministers of the Bishop stands on the Epistle side of the altar, holding a chalice containing wine, and a clean linen cloth in his hands, to whom each one goes, takes a little of the purification, wipes his mouth, and retires to his place.

All having received the purification, the Bishop rubs the paten over his chalice, washes his fingers over it, also takes the ablution, receives the mitre, and washes his hands. Meanwhile the new priests say with the Bishop:

Grant, Lord, that what we have taken with our mouth, we may receive with a pure mind, that of a temporal

Sanguis Dómini nostri Jesu Christi, custódiat ánimam meam in vitam ætérnam. Amen.

Postquam Pontifex se communicavit, Ordinati ad Presbyteratum consurgunt et accedunt ad altare, et Pontifex eos communicat, proferens formulam:

Corpus Domini nostri Jesu Christi custodiat te in vitam æternam.

Unusquisque respondet, *Amen*, osculatur manum Pontificis, et recipit Sacram Particulam.

Postea reliqui Ordinati genuflexi ante altare, dicunt *Confiteor*, submissa voce, cui Pontifex adjicit pro more, "Misereatur," etc., et "Indulgentiam," etc., et communicat eos, dicens eamdem formulam ac pro Presbyteris.

Unus ministrorum Pontificis stat juxta cornu Epistolæ altaris calicem habens cum vino, et mappulam mundam in manibus, ad quem singuli communicati accedunt, et se purificant, os extergunt, et ad partem se locant.

Omnibus purificatis, Pontifex extergit patenam super calicem suum, super eum digitos abluit, sumit ablutionem, accípit mitram et lavat manus. Interim dicunt cum Pontifice Novi Presbyteri:

Quod ore súmpsimus, Dómine, pura mente capiámus: et de múnere temporáli fiat nobis remédium sempitér-

gift it may become to us an eternal remedy. May thy body, O Lord, which I have received, and thy blood, which I have drunk, cleave to my bowels; and grant that no stain of sin may remain in me, who have been nourished with thy pure and holy sacrament. Who livest and reignest for ever and ever. Amen.

The Bishop, having washed his hands, takes off his mitre, and standing on the Epistle side of the altar, reads the following Responsory:

I will not call you servants, but my friends; because everything that I have done in your midst has been made known to you. Alleluia.

Receive the Holy Ghost, the Paraclete, in you. He it is whom the Father will send to you. Alleluia.

V. You are my friends if you do the things that I command you. Receive, &c.

V. Glory be to the Father, and to the Son, and to the Holy Ghost,

He it is whom, &c.

Meanwhile the new priests rise and stand before the altar.

num. Corpus tuum, Dómine, quod sumpsi, et Sanguis, quem potávi, adhæreat viscéribus meis: et præsta, ut in me non remáneat scélerum mácula, quem pura, et sancta refecérunt Sacraménta. Qui vivis et regnas in sæcula sæculórum. Amen.

Pontifex, lotis manibus, mitra deposita, stans in cornu Epistolæ altaris legit Responsorium.

Jam non dicam vos servos, sed amícos meos, quia ómnia cognovístis, quæ operátus sum in médio vestri. Allelúia.

Accípite Spíritum sanctum in vobis Paráclitum. Ille est, quem Pater mittet vobis. Allelúia.

V. Vos amíci mei estis, si fecéritis, quæ ego præcípio vobis. Accípite, etc.

V. Glória Patri, et Fílio, et Spirítui sancto.

Ille est, quem, etc.

Interim assurgunt Novi Presbyteri et stant ante altare.

After reading the Responsory, the Bishop having received his mitre, turns towards the priests ordained, who standing in front of him before the altar, profess the faith they are about to preach, saying:

I believe in God the Father Almighty, Creator of heaven and earth, and in Jesus Christ his only son our Lord; who was conceived by the Holy Ghost, born of the Virgin Mary, suffered under Pontius Pilate, was crucified, dead and buried; he descended into hell; the third day he rose again from the dead, he ascended into heaven, sitteth at the right hand of God the Father Almighty; from thence he shall come to judge the living and the dead. I believe in the Holy Ghost; the Holy Catholic Church; the communion of saints; the forgiveness of sins; the resurrection of the body; and life everlasting. Amen.

Then the Bishop with his mitre on, sitting on the faldstool before the middle of the altar, places both hands on the head of each of the new priests kneeling before him, saying to each:

Receive the Holy Ghost; whose sins you shall forgive, they are forgiven

Lecto Responsorio, Pontifex, accepta mitra, vertit se ad Presbyteros ordinatos, qui ante altare coram ipso stantes, profitentur fidem quam prædicaturi sunt, dicentes :

Credo in Deum, Patrem omnipoténtem, Creatórem cœli et terræ. Et in Jesum Christum Fílium ejus únicum, Dóminum nostrum. Qui concéptus est de Spíritu sancto, natus ex María Vírgine, passus sub Póntio Piláto, crucifíxus, mórtuus, et sepúltus : descéndit ad ínferos ; tértia die resurréxit a mortuis : ascéndit ad cœlos, sedet ad déxteram Dei Patris omnipoténtis. Inde ventúrus est judicáre vivos, et mórtuos. Credo in Spíritum sanctum ; sanctam Ecclésiam Cathólicam ; Sanctórum communiónem ; remissiónem peccatórum ; carnis resurrectiónem ; vitam ætérnam. Amen.

Quo finito, Pontifex cum mitra sedens super faldistorium, ante medium altaris, imponit ambas manus super capita singulorum coram eo genuflectentium, dicens cuilibet :

Accipe Spíritum sanctum, quorum

them, and whose sins you shall retain, they are retained.

Then unfolding the chasuble of each, which is gathered up on the shoulders, he lets it fall, saying:

May the Lord clothe thee with the stole of innocence.

After this the new priest places his hands joined between those of the Bishop, who says to each, if he be his Ordinary:

Dost thou promise to me and my successors reverence and obedience?

And each one answers:

I promise.

But if the Bishop is not his Ordinary, he says to each secular priest, while he holds his hands between his own, "Dost thou promise to the Bishop, thy Ordinary," &c.; and to each Regular, "Dost thou promise to the Prelate, thy Ordinary," &c.

Dost thou promise to the Bishop (or the Prelate), thy Ordinary for the time being, reverence and obedience?

And each one answers:

I promise.

Then the Bishop holding his hands between his own, kisses each one on the right cheek, saying:

The peace of the Lord be always with thee.

And he answers:

Amen.

remíseris peccáta, remittúntur eis : et quorum retinúeris, reténta sunt.

> Deinde explicans casulam, quam unusquisque habet super humeros complicatam, induit illa quemlibet, singulis dicens :

Stola innocéntiæ índuat te Dóminus.

> Post hæc Ordinatus ponit manus suas junctas inter manus Pontificis dicentis cuilibet, si suus est Ordinarius :

Promittis mihi, et successóribus meis reveréntiam, et obediéntiam ?

> Et ille respondet :

Promítto.

> Si vero Pontifex non est suus Ordinarius, cum manus eorum inter suas tenet, ut prefertur, dicit singulis Presbyteris sæcularibus: *Promittis Pontífici Ordinário tuo*, etc. Singulis Regularibus, *Promittis Præláto Ordinário tuo*, etc.

Promittis Pontífici, (vel Præláto) Ordinário tuo, pro témpore exsténti, reveréntiam, et obediéntiam ?

> Et ille respondet :

Promítto.

> Tunc Pontifex tenens manus illius inter suas, osculatur unumquemque in dextera vultus parte dicens :

Pax Dómini sit semper tecum.

> Et ille respondet :

Amen.

After this the new priests return to their places, and the Bishop, sitting with his mitre on and crosier in his hand, exhorts them, saying:

Inasmuch, dearest children, as you are quite liable to err in that in which you are about to engage, I advise you before celebrating Mass, to learn carefully from experienced priests the order of the whole Mass, and everything relating to the consecration, breaking and communion of the Host.

The Bishop rises, and with his mitre on and holding his crosier, he blesses the priests still kneeling before him, saying:

May the blessing of Almighty God, Father, Son and Holy Ghost, descend upon you, that you may be blessed in the priestly order, and may offer propitiatory sacrifices for the sins and offences of the people, to Almighty God, to whom is honor and glory forever and ever. Amen.

It is to be observed that, at this blessing, only the new priests to whom it is given should be kneeling.

After this the Bishop goes to the Missal, and con-

His expletis, et eis ad ordinem suum reversis, Pontifex sedens cum mitra, et baculo, admonet eos, dicens:

Quia res, quam tractatúri estis, satis periculósa est, fílii dilectíssimi, móneo vos, ut diligénter totíus Missæ órdinem, atque Hóstiæ consecratiónem, ac fractiónem, et communiónem, ab áliis jam doctis Sacerdótibus discátis, priúsquam ad celebrándum Missam accedátis.

Pontifex surgit cum mitra, et baculo, et Presbyteris coram eo adhuc genuflexis benedicit, dicens voce competenti:

Benedictio Dei omnipoténtis Pa☩tris, et Fí☩lii et Spíritus☩sancti descéndat super vos: ut sitis benedícti in órdine sacerdotáli; et offerátis placábiles hóstias pro peccátis, atque offensiónibus pópuli omnipoténti Deo, cui est honor, et glória per ómnia sæcula sæculórum. ℟. Amen.

Notandum, quod ad benedictionem istam genuflexi esse debent soli Presbyteri, quibus impertitur.

Post hæc, Pontifex accedit ad Missale, et prosequi-

tinues the Mass with those ordained to the Priesthood.

The Communion.*

He hath rejoiced as a giant to run the way; his going out is from the end of heaven, and his circuit even to the end thereof.

Then the new priests say with the Bishop:

The Lord be with you.

℞. And with thy spirit.

The Post Communion.*

Let us pray.

We beseech thee, O Lord our God, that thou wouldst make these sacred mysteries, which thou hast given us, strengthen in us the effects of our reparation, and be a remedy to us, both now and hereafter.

For those Ordained.

Whom thou, O Lord, refreshest by thy sacraments, benignly support by thy continuing assistance, so that both by these mysteries and by our manner of life, we may obtain the benefits of

---

* See note, page 77.

tur Missam una cum ordinatis ad Presbyteratum:

Communio.*

Exultavit ut gigas ad curréndam viam ; a summo cœlo egréssio ejus, et occúrsus ejus usque ad summum ejus.

Deinde cum Episcopo dicunt :

Dóminus vobíscum.

℞. Et cum spíritu tuo.

Postcommunio.*

Orémus.

Quæsumus Dómine Deus noster, ut sacrosáncta mystéria, quæ pro reparatiónis nostræ munímine contulísti ; et præsens nobis remédium esse fácias, et futúrum.

Pro Ordinatis.

Quos tuis, Dómine, réficis Sacraméntis, contínuis attólle benígnus auxíliis ; ut tuæ redemptiónis efféctum, et mystériis capiámus, et móribus. Qui vivis et regnas cum Deo Patre in unitáte

---

* Vide not. pag. 77.

thy redemption. Who with God the Father and the Holy Ghost, livest and reignest one God, for ever and ever. Amen.

Other Post-Communions.

Of the B. V. M.

Let us pray.

Pour forth, we beseech thee, O Lord, thy grace into our hearts, that we, to whom the incarnation of Christ thy Son, has been made known by the message of an angel, may, by his Passion and Cross, be brought to the glory of his resurrection.

Against the persecutors of the Church.

O Lord, our God! we beseech thee to protect those, whom thou hast permitted to partake of these divine mysteries, from the dangers incident to human life. Through our Lord Jesus Christ thy Son, who with thee and the Holy Ghost, livest and reignest one God for ever and ever. Amen.

Spíritus sancti Deus. Per ómnia sæcula sæculórum. Amen.

Aliæ Postcommuniones
De Sancta Maria.

Orémus.

Gratiam tuam, quæsumus Dómine, mentibus nostris infúnde: ut qui, Angelo nuntiánte, Christi Fílii tui incarnatiónem cognóvimus; per passiónem ejus, et crucem, ad resurrectiónis glóriam perducámur.

Contra persecutores Ecclesiæ.

Quæsumus Dómine Deus noster; ut quos divína tríbuis participatióne gaudére, humánis non sinas subjacére perículis. Per Dóminum nostrum Jesum Christum Fílium tuum, qui tecum vivit, et regnat in unitáte Spíritus sancti Deus. Per ómnia sæcula sæculórum.

Or for the Pope.

Let the participation of the divine sacrament protect us, we beseech thee, O Lord! and always save and strengthen thy servant N., whom thou hast appointed Pastor over thy Church, together with the flock entrusted to his charge. Through the same Jesus Christ, thy Son our Lord, who with thee and the Holy Ghost liveth and reigneth God, for ever and ever. Amen.

The Lord be with you.

℞. And with thy spirit.

* Let us bless the Lord.

℞. Thanks be to God.

Then they say:

Let this acknowledgment of my subjection, O holy Trinity! be pleasing to thee, and grant that this sacrifice which I, though unworthy, have offered to thy divine Majesty, may be acceptable to thee, and through thy mercy be propitiatory for me, and for all

---

* Or, "So Mass is ended."

Vel pro Papa.

Hæc nos, quæsumus Dómine, divíni Sacraménti percéptio prótegat: et fámulum tuum N. quem Pastórem Ecclésiæ tuæ præésse voluísti, una cum commísso sibi grege salvet semper, et múniat. Per Dóminum nostrum Jesum Christum Fílium tuum: qui tecum vivit, et regnat in unitáte Spíritus sancti Deus. Per ómnia sæcula sæculórum.

Dóminus vobíscum.

℞. Et cum spíritu tuo.

* Benedicámus Dómino.

℞. Deo grátias.

Deinde dicunt:

Placeat tibi, sancta Trínitas, obséquium servitútis meæ et præsta: ut Sacrifícium, quod óculis tuæ Majestátis indígnus óbtuli, tibi sit acceptábile, mihíque, et ómnibus, pro quibus illud óbtuli, sit, te miseránte, propit-

---
* Vel *Ita Missa est.*

those for whom it has been offered. Through Christ our Lord. Amen.

Here the Bishop, having received his mitre and crosier, gives the usual blessing.
Then he sits, and thus addresses all those who have received orders and who kneel before the altar.

Most beloved children, consider well the Order you have received, and the burden placed upon your shoulders: strive to lead a holy and religious life, and to please Almighty God, that you may be able to obtain his grace, which may He, through His mercy, vouchsafe to grant you.

Each of you promoted to first Tonsure, or to the four Minor Orders, say once the seven Penitential Psalms, with the Litany of the Saints, the versicles, and prayers.

You who have been ordained to Subdeaconship or Deaconship say a Nocturn of this day.*

You who have been ordained to Priesthood, after your first Mass say three other Masses, to wit, one of the Holy Ghost, another of the Blessed

---

* Or the Bishop may assign a nocturn of another day.

iábile. Per Christum Dóminum nostrum. Amen.

Quo dicto Pontifex, accepta mitra et baculo Pastorali, dat benedictionem solitam.

Tum sedet, et alloquitur omnes Ordinatos, ante altare genuflexos, sub his verbis:

Fílii dilectíssimi, diligénter considerate Ordinem per vos suscéptum, ac onus húmeris vestris impósitum; studéte sancte et religióse vívere, atque omnipoténti Deo placére, ut grátiam suam possítis acquírere, quam ipse vobis per suam misericórdiam concédere dignétur.

Sínguli ad primam Tonsúram, vel ad quatuor minóres Ordines promóti, dícite semel septem Psalmos pænitentiáles, cum Litániis, Versículis, et Oratiónibus. Ad Subdiaconátum, vel Diaconátum, Noctúrnum talis diéi.* Ad Presbyterátum vero ordináti, post primam vestram Missam, tres álias Missas, vidélicet, unam de Spíri-

---

* *i. e.*, hujus diei. Vel Episcopus nocturnum alterius diei designare potest.

Mary ever Virgin, and a third for the faithful departed, and also pray to Almighty God for me.

Then the Bishop turns toward the altar, and says with those ordained to the Priesthood:

The Lord be with you.

℟. And with thy spirit.

The beginning of the Gospel according to St. John.

In the beginning was the Word, and the Word was with God, and the Word was God. The same was in the beginning with God. All things were made by him, and without him was made nothing that was made. In him was life, and the life was the light of men; and the light shineth in darkness, and the darkness did not comprehend it.

There was a man sent from God, whose name was John. This man came for a witness, to give testimony of the light, that all men might believe through him. He was not the light, but was to give testimony of the light. That was the true light which enlight-

tu sancto, áliam de beáta María semper Vírgine, tértiam pro Fidélibus defúnctis dícite, et omnipoténtem Deum étiam pro me oráte.

Tum Pontifex convertit se ad altare, et dicit cum ordinatis ad Presbyteratum:

Dóminus vobíscum.

℟. Et cum spíritu tuo.

Inítium sancti Evangélii secúndum Jóannem.

In princípio erat Verbum, et Verbum erat apud Deum, et Deus erat Verbum. Hoc erat in princípio apud Deum. Omnia per ipsum facta sunt: Et sine ipso factum est nihil quod factum est. In ipso vita erat, et vita erat lux hóminum: et lux in ténebris lucet, et ténebræ eam non comprehendérunt. Fuit homo missus a Deo: cui nomen erat Joánnes. Hic venit in testimónium, ut testimónium perhibéret de lúmine, ut omnes créderent per illum. Non erat ille lux, sed ut testimónium perhibéret de lúmine. Erat lux vera

eneth every man that cometh into this world. He was in the world, and the world was made by him, and the world knew him not. He came unto his own, and his own received him not. But as many as received him, to them he gave power to be made the sons of God, to them that believe in his name; who are born, not of blood, nor of the will of the flesh, nor of the will of man, but of God. [Here kneel down.] *And the Word was made flesh*, and dwelt among us; and we saw his glory, the glory as it were, of the only begotten of the Father, full of grace and truth.

℟. Thanks be to God.

After Mass the following hymn may be sung in thanksgiving.

The Bishop intones it in a loud voice, and it is sung by the choir, while he takes off the Pontifical vestments.

Thee, sov'reign God, our grateful accents praise;
We own thee Lord, and bless thy wondrous ways.

quæ illúminat omnem hóminem veniéntem in hunc mundum: In mundo erat, et mundus per ipsum factus est, et mundus eum non cognóvit. In própria venit, et sui eum non recepérunt. Quotquot autem recepérunt eum, dedit eis potestátem fílios Dei fíeri, his, qui credunt in nómine ejus: qui non ex sanguínibus, neque ex voluntáte carnis, neque ex voluntáte viri, sed ex Deo nati sunt. [Hic genuflectitur.] *Et verbum caro factum est*, et habitávit in nobis; et vídimus glóriam ejus, glóriam quasi unigéniti a Patre, plenum grátiæ, et veritátis.

℞. Deo grátias.

Post Missam cantari potest Hymnus sequens in gratiarum actionem.

Pontifex incipit alta voce et cantatur a choro dum paramenta Pontificalia dimittit.

Te Deum laudámus: Te Dominum confitémur.

Te ætérnum Pátrem omnis terra venerátur.

To thee, eternal Father, earth's whole frame,
With loudest trumpets sounds immortal fame.
Lord God of Hosts! to thee the heavenly powers,
With sounding anthems fill thy vaulted tow'rs.
The Cherubim thrice Holy, Holy, Holy, cry:
Thrice Holy all the Seraphim reply,
And thrice returning echoes, endless song supply.
Both heaven and earth thy Majesty display;
They owe their beauty to thy glorious ray.
Thy praises fill the loud apostles' choir:
The train of prophets in the song conspire.
Legions of martyrs in the chorus shine,
And vocal blood with vocal music join,
By these thy Church, inspir'd with heav'nly art,
Around the world maintains a second part;

Tibi omnes Angeli, tibi cœli et univérsæ potestátes.

Tibi Chérubim et Séraphim, incessábili voce proclámant.

Sanctus, Sanctus, Sanctus Dóminus Deus Sábaoth,

Pléni sunt cœli et térra majestátis glóriæ tuæ.

Te gloriósus Apostolórum chorus;
Te Prophetárum laudabilis númerus;
Te Mártyrum candidátus laudat exércitus.

Te per orbem terrárum, sancta confitétur Ecclésia

Pátrem imménsæ majestátis.

Venerándum tuum vérum et únicum Fílium,

Sanctum quoque paráclitum Spíritum.
Tu Rex glóriæ Christe.
Tu Pátris sempitérnus es Fílius.

And tunes her sweetest notes, O God! to thee,
The Father of unbounded Majesty;
The Son, ador'd co-partner of thy seat,
And equal everlasting Paraclete.
Thou king of glory, Christ, of the Most High,
Thou co-eternal filial Deity:
Thou who to save the world's impending doom,
Vouchsaf'dst to dwell within a virgin's womb:
Old tyrant Death, disarm'd; before thee flew
The bolts of heav'n, and back the foldings drew
To give access, and make the faithful way;
From God's right hand thy filial beams display.
Thou art to judge the living and the dead.
* Then spare those souls for whom thy veins have bled.
O take us up among the blest above,

---

* This verse is sung kneeling.

Tu ad liberandum susceptúrus hóminem, non horruísti Vírginis úterum.

Tu devícto mortis acúleo, aperuísti credéntibus régna cœlorum.

Tu ad déxteram Dei sédes in glória Patris.

Judex créderis esse ventúrus:

* Te ergo, quæsumus, tuis fámulis súbveni, quos pretióso sánguine redemísti.

Ætérna fac cum Sanctis tuis in gloria numerári.

Sálvum fac pópulum tuum, Domine: et benedic hereditáti tuæ.

Et rege eos, et extólle illos usque in ætérnum.

Per síngulos díes benedícimus te.

Et laudámus nomen tuum in sæculum, et in sæculum sæculi.

---

* Hic versus dicitur flexisgenibus.

To share with them thy everlasting love,
Preserve, O Lord, thy people, and enhance
Thy blessing on thine own inheritance.
For ever raise their hearts and rule their ways;
Each day we bless thee, and proclaim thy praise:
No age shall fail to celebrate thy name;
Nor hour neglect thy everlasting fame.
Preserve our souls, O Lord, this day from ill:
Have mercy on us, Lord! have mercy still.
As we have hop'd do thou reward our pain:
We've hop'd in thee, let not our hope be vain.

Then the Bishop says the versicles and the prayer.

V. Blessed art thou, O Lord, the God of our fathers.

℟. And worthy of praise, and glorious forever.

Dignáre, Domine, die isto sine peccáto nos custodíre.

Miserére nostri, Domine, miserére nostri.

Fíat misericórdia tua, Dómine, super nos: quemádmodum sperávimus in te.

In te Dómine sperávi: non confúndar in ætérnum.

Deinde Pontifex dicit versiculos et orationem.

V. Benedíctus es Dómine Deus pátrum nostrórum.

℞. Et laudábilis et gloriósus in sæcula.

V. Let us bless the Father, and the Son, and the Holy Ghost.

R. Let us praise and exalt him above all forever.

V. Blessed art thou in the firmament of heaven.

R. And worthy to be praised and glorified and exalted above all forever.

V. Bless the Lord, O my soul.

R. And never forget all he hath done for thee.

V. O Lord, hear my prayer.

R. And let my cry come unto thee.

V. The Lord be with you.

R. And with thy spirit.

Let us pray.

O God, whose mercies are without number, and the treasure of whose goodness is infinite, we give thee thanks for the blessings thou hast bestowed on us; always beseeching thy divine Majesty, that as thou grantest what we ask, so thou wouldst continue thy favors to us in such a manner, that

V. Benedicámus Pátrem et Fílium cum sáncto Spíritu.

℟. Laudémus et superexaltémus eum in sæcula.

V. Benedíctus es Dómine in firmaménto cœli.

℟. Et laudábilis et gloriósus et superexaltátus in sæcula.

V. Benedic anima mea Dómino.

℟. Et noli oblivísci ómnes retributiónes ejus.

V. Dómine exáudi oratiónem méam.

℟. Et clamor meus ad te véniat.

V. Dóminus vobíscum.

℟. Et cum spíritu tuo.

Orémus.

Deus cujus misericórdiæ non est númerus, et bonitátis infinítus est thesáurus; piíssimæ majestáti tuæ pro collátis dónis grátias ágimus, tuam sémper cleméntiam exorántes; ut qui peténtibus postuláta concédis, eósdem

by them we may be prepared for receiving the rewards of eternal happiness. Through Christ our Lord. Amen.

The Bishop with his ministers leaves the church, and afterwards, two by two, all who have received orders, the new priests going first.

non desérens, ad præmia futúra dispónas. Per Christum Dóminum nostrum. Amen.

Pontifex cum ministris de Ecclesia discedit ; deinde Ordinati, bini et bini, præcedentibus Novis Presbyteris.

www.ingramcontent.com/pod-product-compliance
Lightning Source LLC
Chambersburg PA
CBHW031815220426
43662CB00007B/659